THE ARMADA IN THE PUBLIC RECORDS

I.   *The Spanish Fleet off the Coast of Cornwall, 29 July.*

The Pine engravings of the House of Lords Armada Tapestries. John Pine, London, 1739.
NMM (this frontispiece and the following similar pictures II–X).

Cover: The Spanish Armada. English School,
16th century. Reproduced by permission of
the Society of Apothecaries.

THE
Armada
IN THE
PUBLIC RECORDS

N A M Rodger

LONDON HER MAJESTY'S STATIONERY OFFICE

CONTENTS

HMSO publications are available from:

HMSO Publications Centre
(Mail and telephone orders only)
PO Box 276, London, SW8 5DT
Telephone orders 01-622 3316
General enquiries 01-211 5656
(queuing system in operation for both numbers)

HMSO Bookshops
49 High Holborn, London, WC1V 6HB
01-211 5656 (Counter service only)

258 Broad Street, Birmingham, B1 2HE
021-643 3740

Southey House, 33 Wine Street, Bristol, BS1 2BQ
(0272) 264306

9-21 Princess Street, Manchester, M60 8AS
061-834 7201

80 Chichester Street, Belfast, BT1 4JY
(0232) 238451

71 Lothian Road, Edinburgh, EH3 9AZ
031-228 4181

HMSO's Accredited Agents
(see Yellow Pages)

and through good booksellers

Preface

As the archives of the English government, the Public Records naturally contain many thousands of documents about the defence of the country against the Spanish Armada of 1588. Although there are important collections of manuscripts relating to the Armada elsewhere, and of course the English documents do not present the Spanish side of the campaign, there is no other source remotely as rich in records of the campaign. This little book attempts to give a brief narrative of the Armada fighting and what lay behind it, together with a selection of documents, in transcript and facsimile, chosen to give a flavour of the originals.

The Spanish Armada

England and Spain were not natural enemies in the late sixteenth century. France and Spain, being the great powers of western Europe, were generally at odds; for reasons of proximity and rival dynastic claims France and England had long been rivals, and recently been at war. This made England and Spain potential allies in the same way as France and Scotland were. There were strong and ancient trade links between the two kingdoms. Moreover King Philip II of Spain had formerly been King Philip I of England, the consort of Queen Mary, and seems to have retained much knowledge of, and some affection for his old kingdom. It is true that the establishment of a reformed church in England was bound to upset the champion of Catholicism, but in the 1580s religion was not yet by itself the cause of war among Christians. The only serious religious wars in Europe were the intermittent struggle against the infidel Turk which had occupied Christendom for centuries, and the civil war in France which was at least as much dynastic as religious.

II. The Spanish and English Fleets near Plymouth, 30-31 July.

To this might have been added the rebellion of the Spanish Netherlands, and in particular of the northern provinces in which Calvinism was most strongly established. Philip II was the legitimate ruler of almost all of what is now the Netherlands and Belgium, but by the early 1580s the northern provinces had won a precarious independence, perpetually threatened by the powerful Spanish army of the Duke of Parma, based in Brussels. Parma's force was by modern standards an undisciplined rabble, ill-clothed, generally unpaid, often mutinous and sometimes starving, but by the standards of sixteenth-century Europe it was the finest professional army in the world, viewed by its actual and potential enemies with awe and terror. The general introduction of bastioned fortifications had made it very hard for even the best army to make rapid conquests, but Parma's force was the best army, and in the early 1580s it was making steady progress against the Dutch rebels. By 1585 it seemed that the great rebellion might be on the point of extinction.

Across the Channel, Queen Elizabeth and her advisers viewed this process with mixed emotions. They were naturally sympathetic to the cause of reformed religion struggling for survival against resurgent Catholicism, but few of them - certainly not the Queen - felt undue warmth for Calvinism and republicanism, or for rebels against their rightful sovereign. For the English government, however, the strategic consideration outweighed all others. If the greatest military power in Europe, possessed of the finest professional army, should hold the Low Countries without challenge, then England's freedom of action, if not her independence, would be gravely threatened. What was worse France was quite unable to act in her usual role of a counterpoise to Spanish power, being distracted by a civil war in which the dominant party, the Catholic League of the Dukes of Guise, was heavily subsidised by Spain.

For these reasons, the English government in 1585 signed the Treaty of Nonsuch with the Dutch rebels, promising them limited military and financial assistance. Queen Elizabeth's object was to give the Dutch just enough support to prevent their defeat, and if possible to enforce some sort of compromise which would leave neither party dangerously dominant in the Low Countries. She certainly did not believe that outright Dutch victory against Spain was possible, nor from England's point of view was it desirable, and she had no intention of provoking direct war between Spain and England. Her kingdom was by far the poorer and weaker of the two, and it would have been folly to risk a war from which England had nothing to gain.

Unfortunately for Elizabeth, King Philip saw the situation differently. English assistance, though not very considerable, was indeed just enough to check Parma's advance in the Netherlands, and within a few months of the Treaty of Nonsuch he ordered plans to be drawn up for an invasion of England. If English help alone kept the Dutch rebels going, then the elimination of England seemed to be the key to triumph in northern Europe. When Elizabeth in a further attempt to deter Spain allowed Drake to sail on a large-scale raid to the Caribbean late in 1585, it only hardened Spanish determination and accelerated the drift to war. By 1586 most observers thought that it would be very difficult to avoid full-scale war, and the English were aware that Spain was already assembling the elements of an invasion fleet. In 1587 Drake was again allowed to sail on a raid, this time to the coasts of Spain itself, where he was able to enter Cadiz harbour and sink or capture a considerable volume of shipping intended for the invasion fleet, besides stopping all shipping on the Algarve coast and taking a rich merchantman in the Azores. It looks as though Elizabeth still had some hopes that such a raid might persuade Spain to a compromise: Drake and King Philip, who in this matter were of one mind, saw it as the opening battle of the forthcoming invasion campaign.

At the same time as Drake was burning Spanish shipping and supplies, Anglo-Spanish negotiations were actually in progress in the Low Countries between emissaries of the Queen and the Duke of Parma. On the Spanish side it seems fairly clear that they had been undertaken as a blind, at a point when war with England was already determined on.

2

Elizabeth and some, though not all of her councillors, were not without hope that a compromise peace might be possible, and discussions continued until the Armada was actually sighted in the Channel. King Philip apparently continued to regard the negotiations as a deception, but it is curious to see that Parma, far from Madrid, close to the military situation and obliged to run a semi-independent foreign policy, came to look on them in much the same light as the Queen, and hoped to gain by negotiation more than there seemed much chance of winning on the battlefield. These hopes were destroyed by his master's insistence on hazarding all on a victory at sea.

Why he did so, at the time and in the manner which he did, is one of the great unanswerable questions about the Armada campaign. King Philip was an intelligent monarch, personally familiar with the geography of England and the Low Countries (in both of which he had lived), well informed on every aspect of the strategic situation, and yet he insisted, against the objections of Parma and most of his advisers, on a plan which was radically unsound. At the root of his difficulty was the separation of the different parts of the Spanish empire: vast and powerful though it was, its scattered domains in the Iberian peninsula, in Italy, in Flanders and in the New World could only be linked together by sea. In particular, communications between Spain and Flanders were difficult by land, and virtually impossible by sea. In 1572 the Dutch rebels had captured the Spanish North Sea naval base at Veere and put their nothern squadron out of action; since then Parma had recaptured part of the North Sea coast with the ports of Dunkirk and Sluys, but he had not yet re-established any effective naval forces. The shallow coastal waters of Flanders and Zealand were dominated by the Dutch fleet of small 'flyboats', commanded by Justin of Nassau. The only deep-water port which might have accommodated a large fleet from

III.　　*The English Engage the Spanish Fleet near Plymouth, 31 July.*

Spain, Flushing in Zealand, was firmly held by the Dutch and an English garrison, and Parma was at best some years' campaigning away from any hope of taking it. This made it practically impossible for Parma's army, however near and threatening to England it seemed to be, to attempt an invasion. The troops could be loaded into barges and lighters, but so long as Parma had no powerful coastal squadrons of his own, he had no chance of safely crossing the shallows of the Zealand banks where the Dutch flyboats cruised. Regardless of what English or Spanish navies might do in the deep water further offshore, the Duke of Parma's army was effectively neutralised by the Dutch navy.

This crucial fact King Philip's plan ignored. His great fleet carried at most 17,000 troops (figures differ) and a siege train, a force considered inadequate to conquer England, and it sailed under orders absolutely forbidding it to undertake any landing, or even to engage in any naval battle not forced upon it, until it had met and escorted Parma's invasion force. How the two forces were to meet when the big ships could not cross the Zealand Banks and Parma had no harbour to offer them, was not explained. This contradiction alone would be sufficient to explain the failure of the Armada. The only ways to resolve it would have been either to postpone the enterprise of England, and concentrate all resources on the campaign in Flanders until Parma could capture Flushing and re-open sea communications with Spain; or to mount an independent invasion from Spain, large enough to land in England without the assistance of Parma's army. The second had been the choice of the Marquis of Santa Cruz, Spain's greatest admiral, who in March 1586 presented King Philip with his detailed plan for the invasion of England. It called for 60,000 soldiers, 30,000 seamen and 77,000 tons of shipping - figures so enormous that not just the Spanish empire but the whole resources of Christendom would scarcely have sufficed to provide them. Any fleet within the power of Spain to put to sea must be considerably smaller and weaker than that, from which it seemed to follow that the necessary forces could only be found by including Parma's army in the scheme. The Enterprise of England was for the defence of the Catholic faith and consequently must enjoy God's favour: He would have to make it possible for fleet and army to join hands. In that confidence Philip ordered the Armada to sail, and with no more confidence than that, it seems, his officers took their orders and set out to do their duty.

So perilous did the expedition appear that some historians have doubted if it was ever seriously intended to invade, as opposed to deter. It has been suggested that the Armada was nothing but a massive show of force intended to cow the English into submission without fighting. If so vast sums of money were wasted equipping it with items of no practical use and its senior officers were deliberately deceived as to its real objects, which would have been a recipe for an expensive disaster ill-calculated to impress the English or anyone else. There is no reason to doubt that Philip did really intend his fleet and army to invade England and impose terms on Elizabeth. His minimum demands were, in order of importance: toleration for English Catholics, withdrawal of English support for the Dutch rebels, and payment of an indemnity. The overthrow of Queen Elizabeth, the restoration of Catholicism as the religion of all Englishmen, the addition of England to the Spanish empire, were not in the programme. All these things were feared by the English, and doubtless they would all have been welcome in Madrid, but not even the most optimistic Spanish planner thought them very likely. The presence of a large body of the finest troops in the world on English soil, threatening London if not actually occupying it, would almost certainly have been enough to bring to terms an English government which possessed no regular army at all; to that extent the Spanish plan was sound. The difficulty was to get the famous Spanish infantry ashore.

Indeed, before that problem could be faced there was another, even more acute, to be overcome: getting the troops to sea. Putting fleets to sea was the most complex, technically demanding and expensive task a sixteenth-century state could undertake, a feat equivalent to putting a man on the moon in the twentieth century, and even wealthy Spain was ill-

4

equipped to face it. Until the conquest of Portugal in 1580 Spain had had no ocean-going navy at all, only her galley squadrons in the Mediterranean. The conquest of Portugal had gained Philip a useful squadron of galleons, but he still had no dockyard and no permanent naval administration. Although Spain was the wealthiest power in Europe, and its military organisation was far in advance of any other power's, its naval effort had to be completely improvised. The process of assembling the fleet began in the spring of 1586, and was still far from complete when Drake's raid on Cadiz in May 1587 caused further delays. Neither Spain herself nor all the Spanish empire could supply the ships, men and guns which were needed; the whole of Europe was scoured by Spanish emissaries trying to charter ships and buy heavy guns. Meanwhile those ships which were assembled were lying fully-manned in the ports of Spain and Portugal, their supplies consuming and their men wasting away with the sickness which inevitably followed in that age when any considerable body of men were crowded together for long. When the Marquis of Santa Cruz died in February 1588 the great fleet, still far from complete, was already sliding into chaos. Moreover it was costing 700,000 ducats a month, or more than four-fifths of the entire revenues of the Spanish empire. Informed observers (notably the Pope, who had a sneaking admiration for Queen Elizabeth, and deeply resented Philip's efforts to reduce him to a Spanish puppet) openly mocked Spain and predicted that the Armada would never sail.

In this desperate situation, with the future strategy and present reputation of the Spanish empire hanging in the balance, the most urgent requirement was for administrative skill. Someone was needed of mature judgement and extensive experience in organising fleets and armies, a man of unequalled rank, credit and influence, who could make up in his own person for the weaknesses of Spanish government. There was only one

IV.   The English Pursue the Spanish Fleet East of Plymouth, 31 July-1 August.

such man: the Duke of Medina Sidonia. The choice has often been derided, and it is true that the Duke was not an experienced admiral, but that was the least of King Philip's requirements in February 1588. Santa Cruz, the finest of Spain's admirals, had presided over deepening chaos; more than sea experience was needed if the Armada was ever to get to sea. That it finally did so is owing almost entirely to the tireless work and organising genius of Medina Sidonia, who almost single-handed supplied the naval administration which the Spanish government lacked.

The annual revenues of Philip II in 1588 were about 10,000,000 ducats or nearly £3,000,000; Queen Elizabeth's at the same date were about £300,000, though unrepeatable wartime taxation swelled them to £400,000 or somewhat more. With little more than a tenth of the resources of Spain, England was attempting to compete in a business which required immense expenditure sustained over long periods. The remarkable thing is that it was precisely in this area of administration, support and supply that the English navy had a decisive advantage. In the first place Queen Elizabeth *had* a navy; a permanent force of fighting ships in her own service. Though not very large by the standards of Mediterranean galley fleets, it was by some way the largest standing navy in northern waters, and it was supported by an administrative system which was, for its day, notably efficient and flexible. The Navy Board, the committee of senior officials who dealt with the maintenance, supply and manning of the fleet, had been established by Henry VIII, but to a considerable extent the English naval system of 1588 was that which had been expanded and perfected during Queen Mary's short reign, and at the instance of her consort, King Philip I of England. Not least of the ironies of 1588 is that Philip was defeated by a fleet which he himself had done much to establish. It was he who made available to his English subjects, still very backward in navigation, the expertise and resources of the *Casa de Contratacion* in Seville which licensed and controlled Spain's overseas trade. It was during his reign, in 1557, that for the first time the English fleet received a permanent 'ordinary' or budget, with which a continuous naval system could be maintained year after year.

The officials who were responsible were the members of the Navy Board, who were in 1588 John Hawkins the Treasurer of the Navy, Sir William Winter the Surveyor of the Queen's Ships and Master of the Ordnance for the Navy, William Borough the Clerk of the Ships, and William Holstock the Controller. All of them were seamen and administrators of long experience: Hawkins was the leading merchant and shipowner of Plymouth, and had been Treasurer for ten years. From 1585 he had undertaken the whole 'Ordinary' maintenance of the Queen's ships by contract for an annual fee of £5,714. Winter was a veteran sea officer who had served continuously for over forty years, and Holstock had served afloat and ashore since Henry VIII's time. Borough was a famous explorer and navigator. Under their charge were the dockyards at Deptford, Chatham and Portsmouth, of which Chatham, where the ships were laid up when out of commission, was rapidly growing to be the most important. James Quarles, one of the officers of the queen's household, had the thankless responsibility of victualling the Navy.

Queen Elizabeth inherited from her half-sister a fleet of about 40 sail, and soon after her accession it was laid down as a policy that 24 ships were always to be kept ready for sea at fourteen days' notice. Moreover a series of increasingly elaborate surveys were undertaken of the kingdom's resources in merchant shipping and seamen, lists were drawn up of the larger and better-armed merchantmen, and arrangements made to requisition them up for service with the Queen's ships in the event of war. This careful planning for rapid mobilization was a remarkable, for the sixteenth century quite unique, policy, and it was one of the keys to the English success in 1588. Elizabeth could not hope to keep so large a fleet in being for so long as Spain did, but what she had she could mobilize at very short notice. Lacking any equivalent administration, the Spaniards were in effect obliged to keep the Armada on a war footing throughout the whole period of two years during which it was assembled, with the inevitable result that for all Medina Sidonia's efforts it eventually sailed sickly, in poor repair and short of many essential supplies.

To achieve even this required prodigious expenditure during the preparations, the crippling of Spain's overseas trade and the suspension of the vital silver fleet to provide shipping for the enterprise. Yet throughout almost all the two years during which the Armada was being made ready, most of the Queen's ships lay at their moorings in the Medway. In the whole year of 1587, while the Armada was costing Philip nearly £200,000 a month, Elizabeth spent only £44,000 on her fleet, of which all but £7,000 went to pay for the squadron which went to Cadiz with Drake. Having made no extraordinary preparations during the autumn of 1587, she was able in December, when threatening intelligence was received, to put a large fleet to sea at a fortnight's notice, and then as swiftly to pay most of it off when the threat receded until the spring. Queen Elizabeth was obliged to adopt this policy because of her penury; the impossibility of raising large loans or deficit finance in the modern style left her no alternative. Philip's wealth allowed him, and Spain's administrative weakness compelled him, to keep a great fleet in being for two years; Elizabeth's poverty permitted her to match that fleet for only a few months. They had to be the right few months, so she could not afford to risk mobilisation unless the threat was immediate, but she could not have afforded to risk delaying mobilization if it had not been possible to put her ships to sea very quickly. Because of the efficiency of the Navy Board, the dockyards, and the victualling organisation she was able to do so. England's very weak resources were deployed to maximum effect, at exactly the right time and place: Spain's vastly greater resources were dissipated in trying to improvise the great fleet without an adequate logistical base.

V.   *The English and Spanish Fleets off Berry Head and the Engagement near Portland Bill, 1-2 August.*

What is more, Spain's lack of a standing navy left her at a serious disadvantage in the quality of her ships. Only the Portuguese galleons and the four Neapolitan galleasses (hybrid galley-galleons) could be described as regular warships, and most of the larger ships of the Armada were decisively inferior to the English ships, especially the newer English ships, in two vital respects: speed and armament. The English had come relatively late to modern shipbuilding, as they had to ocean voyaging, but in the 1570s the Queen's master shipwrights had developed a type of warship which was the equal, if not the superior, of anything afloat. Naval terminology was then in a very undeveloped state and there was no single term for these new ships; they were often referred to as the 'middling sort' or 'second sort' of galleon, because they were in tonnage terms smaller than the big old high-castled types which were still being built into the 1560s, or as 'race-built', in reference to their relatively low superstructure, especially forward. With lower forecastles they were faster and more weatherly than their predecessors, and they carried a much heavier armament. It was galleons of this type which led the English fleet in 1588, and formed its greatest strength. Moreover many of the smaller English ships, down to the little pinnaces of no more than fifty or a hundred tons which were the smallest men-of-war capable of cruising independantly, were built along similar lines and enjoyed similar advantages of speed.

Because even the best Spanish ships were generally slower and less weatherly than the English, they would find it very difficult to force an engagement on their own terms, or avoid one on the enemy's. Moreover, as the most experienced Spanish officers, including Medina Sidonia, knew quite well, the English terms were likely to be an artillery battle out of boarding range, and the Spanish ships carried many fewer guns, especially heavy guns and those of long range, than the English. If it came to a pitched battle, they were bound to be at a severe disadvantage unless they could grapple and board the English ships. At the battle of Terceira in 1582, during the Spanish conquest of the Azores, Santa Cruz had managed to force just such an action, and won a great victory; King Philip's orders clearly assumed that it could be done again. Either the English would run away, or they would accept battle and could be brought to close action. The problem for Medina Sidonia and his officers would be to bring on a battle on Spanish terms when even the best Spanish ships were likely to be inferior in speed and manoeuvreability to the English.

Furthermore much of the Spanish fleet consisted of ill-armed or quite unarmed transports, even slower and clumsier than their escorts, whereas the English ships were all, if not pure warships, then at least vessels designed, armed and accustomed to fight. They were also in much better condition than the Spanish ships. Because of the controversies raised by Hawkins's disappointed rivals about his contract to maintain the Queen's ships, the actual state of repair of these ships was very thoroughly reported on. It is striking the unanimity, indeed the obvious pride and confidence, with which the captains and admirals of the English fleet praised the condition of their ships.

A further advantage enjoyed by the English was in the number and quality of their seamen. Again this was a very recent gain; even twenty years before, Spain would probably have been superior in men with deep-sea experience, and she still had no lack of experienced masters and pilots. Spanish Atlantic trade, however, was the monopoly of a single port, and to make up the ships and men of the Armada it was necessary to scour the coasts of Catholic Europe. English maritime strength was much more broadly based. Though London contributed the bulk of the biggest and best-armed ships to add to the Queen's own, and undoubtedly predominated in numbers of seamen, there were dozens of ports great and small which could and did contribute ships and men to the fight - far more in fact than could be made use of when the English lacked powder and shot for all the ships they had.

So the English fleet which mobilized in the spring of 1588 was by no means weaker than the Spanish Armada. In simple numbers each side had about 130 ships, of which about sixty on each side could be reckoned as fighting ships of some force, but the English ships were in almost every case faster, better armed and in better condition. Captains and admirals were confident in their ships and in themselves, but they did not know when, or indeed if the Armada would sail, and they were not clear how best to employ their own forces. Naval strategy was barely conceived, and the only existing body of professional knowledge which seemed to offer any guidance was military. The obvious analogy seemed to be with an army blocking a ford or bridge by massing along the river-bank, and the first thought of Elizabeth's government (as well as the first assumption of Philip's) was that the main body of the fleet under the Lord Admiral, Lord Howard of Effingham, should on this principle patrol the Straits of Dover opposite the Duke of Parma's army. Here the finest army in Europe was massed nearest to its enemy; surely this must be the crucial point?

The majority of the experienced sea officers, on the other hand, wanted the fleet stationed as far to the westward as possible, which in practice meant at Plymouth. With the prevailing westerly winds, they would there be able to intercept an invasion fleet from Spain before it could reach the South Coast, and still be perfectly placed to attack it anywhere further up Channel if necessary. This view, of which Drake was the leading exponent, was shared by most of the senior commanders, adopted by Howard the commander-in-chief, and eventually accepted by the government to the extent of sending the bulk of the fleet to Plymouth, leaving only a smaller, though still powerful squadron in the Downs.

This still left the English no nearer knowing where or how to fight the Armada, if it came. No one in England had ever seen, let alone fought, a fleet the size of the Armada, and

VI.   Engagement of the English and Spanish Fleets between Portland Bill and the Isle of Wight, 2-3 August.

moreover none of them had ever served in a fleet the size of their own. Many of them had been raiding in the Caribbean or trading in the Mediterranean with little squadrons of five or even ten ships, and in 1587 Drake had commanded as many as seventeen on the Cadiz expedition, but how to handle a force which eventually totalled 130 sail, was a completely new and baffling problem. Moreover the Spaniards knew much more about defending large formations of ships than the English knew about attacking them. Spain had been running convoys from the Caribbean since 1526, since 1543 they had been armed and escorted. By 1588 they had long experience of the organisation and defence of large squadrons. The French, the Algerines and latterly the Dutch had tried and failed to break into these formations, but the English, latecomers to oceanic warfare, had wisely confined themselves to weaker and smaller targets. The English were confident of success partly because they did not realise how formidable was the threat they were about to face.

The epitome of this confidence, and the source of much of it, was Sir Francis Drake, and it is necessary to consider for a moment why the English fleet, like the Spanish, was commanded not by its most distinguished admiral, but by an eminent nobleman of little sea experience. At one level the explanation was obvious: as Lord Admiral of England, Charles, Lord Howard of Effingham had both the right and the duty to take command of the Queen's fleet, and the fact that he could never have been numbered among the many experienced captains and commanders of the day made no difference at all. In a sense the fact that he took his place as commander of the fleet in 1588 is a tribute to the survival of essentially mediaeval ideas of authority. To the modern mind it has often seemed extra-ordinary that Drake, the most famous admiral of his day, the terror and despair of Catholic Europe, should not have been given the command. In fact there were excellent reasons why not. Though Drake had experience of commanding a larger squadron than most of his famous contemporaries, it was still nothing to compare with the English forces assembled in 1588. Moreover, in an age of quarrelsome and touchy captains, he was one of the least tolerant of all. Chivalrous and polite to his enemies, he could be suspicious and overbearing to his immediate subordinates. On his 1587 expedition he had tried to repeat the precedent of his voyage round the world, and hang his second-in-command. It was hardly the conduct which would endear him to a collection of proud, temperamental and undisciplined individuals several of whom were his personal enemies. What was needed was a man of equable temperament and unequalled rank, apt to take advice and able to give orders without offence, a man who could harness and employ the undoubted talents of his captains, not replace them; an Eisenhower rather than a Montgomery. Howard fitted this requirement exactly, and he deserves full credit not only for the successes of 1588, but for the fact that they were not frustrated, as so many Elizabethan naval and military operations were, by indiscipline, quarrels and treachery.

For Howard and his admirals in the spring of 1588, the most pressing question was whether to await the Spaniards, or pre-empt them by attacking first. Drake and other sea commanders, and eventually Howard whom he won to his point of view, proposed to sail with all or most of the fleet to attack and overwhelm the Armada while it was still in harbour, disorganised and divided between several ports, so repeating on a larger scale Drake's success at Cadiz of the previous year. Elizabeth and her advisers, not without a good deal of wavering, were won over, and during the spring the fleet made several attempts to sail for Spain, only to be driven back by contrary winds. Finally Howard sailed from Plymouth on 7th July for a last attempt. The Armada was by now united, but there was still hope of catching it as it put to sea. On 9th the English were almost in sight of the Spanish coasts when a south-westerly gale and shortage of provisions drove them back.

Subsequent naval historians have generally condemned the Queen's caution and applauded Drake's scheme. Undoubtedly it was in principle sound, and if there had been no hope of peace, no doubt that the Armada would sail, and no shortage of ships and money in England, Drake could have been risked on the coast of Spain with good hope of achieving as much or more than he had the previous year, and perhaps of again delaying the Armada by a year. The risks, however, were much greater than he allowed, Spanish power more formidable than it had been twelve months before, and the consequences of defeat, or simply of costly victory, would have gone far to cripple the English fleet. What might have been the results if Drake's strategy had worked and the English fleet had caught the Armada as it sailed from Corunna, its last port, is impossible to say, but it would have required much luck to achieve there what a few weeks later they failed to achieve in the English Channel, to break up the Spanish formation and inflict a decisive defeat. The expenditure of victuals, the inevitable increase of sickness, would certainly have weakened the English fleet, perhaps fatally, and if the Armada had not been defeated, if it had appeared in the Channel in spite of all that Howard and Drake could do, Seymour's squadron in the Straits of Dover was certainly not powerful enough to have stopped it. Given the very slender English resources, Drake's strategy was extremely dangerous. It is hard to avoid the conclusion that his success the previous year had somewhat gone to his head, and that the Queen's caution, however blinkered, was justified. With all her resources stretched to the utmost, Elizabeth could not afford to grasp at so risky a victory. It is not clear how far she clearly understood the strategic issues at stake, but she was by nature cautious, even irresolute, and her advisers understood very clearly how little money they had left. As it was the fleet which fought the Armada in July was barely victualled for the month, and it is not clear what would have happened if Drake had taken most of its slender supplies of food and gunpowder on a spring expedition.

The English fleet returned to Plymouth on 12th July, and at once began refitting and revictualling for sea, determined to take the first opportunity to return to the coasts of

VII.   The Battle off the Isle of Wight, 4 August.

Spain. They were still hard at work when on the afternoon of 19th (Old Style; 29th according to Spanish reckoning) the pinnace *Golden Hind,* one of the screen of small vessels which had been ordered to patrol to the westward, came running into Plymouth Sound with the momentous news that she had sighted the Spanish fleet off the Scillies. The situation was alarming and dangerous. With a fair wind the Spaniards could in principle have run straight into the Sound and caught the English in just such a trap as Drake had designed for them. It was probably the best, indeed the only chance the Spaniards ever had to force a boarding action in which the English ships, for all their speed and firepower, would be overwhelmed by Spanish soldiery. But to take it they would have had to act with great speed and boldness, risking their whole fleet in a narrow and dangerous inlet from which many of them could scarcely have escaped without a change of wind, and they would have had to disobey King Philip's most explicit orders. It does not appear that they seriously contemplated doing so, at least without more information than they had of the strength and whereabouts of the English fleet, and if they had done it would not have availed, for the English had escaped before the trap could have been sprung. As soon as the ebb began to run, after dark on the same evening that the news was brought, the English ships began to warp out of the Cattewater and down the Sound, towing behind their boats and pinnaces into the teeth of the wind. By morning the bulk of the English fleet was beating out of the Sound, and in the early afternoon Howard sighted the Spaniards, still far off to windward. That night the whole English fleet succeeded in working to windward of the Armada; Howard with the main body to seaward, a smaller squadron (probably the last to get out of Plymouth) beating up between the Spaniards and the shore. By morning the Spaniards had lost the great advantage which chance had initially given them, the weather gage. Now the

VIII. The Voyage to Calais, 4-6 August.

12

English were to windward, with their faster and more weatherly ships, and the Spaniards had lost for good the chance to force close action.

This morning was the first time the two fleets saw each other properly, and it was the first time that each discovered about the other an unpleasant and unexpected fact. For the Spaniards, or at least for most of them, it must have been alarming and astonishing to find with what ease the English ships had escaped from the trap and recovered the weather gage, and to see with their own eyes how slender were Spanish chances of catching even such small forces as the inshore squadron. It seems at daybreak to have been within gunshot of the Spanish van and all but trapped against the land, but beat away to windward to rejoin Howard with no apparent difficulty. For the English the morning showed them for the first time the formidable strength of Spanish military discipline at sea. The Armada then took up, and must long have practised, a precise defensive formation, with the heaviest fighting ships disposed ahead and on either quarter, and the main body of transports gathered in the centre. It was impossible for the English to mount an effective attack on the Armada as a whole without breaking up this formation, and to do this they had to scatter either or both of the 'wings', the fighting squadrons which now took up position on the quarters of the Spanish fleet. The conception and execution of such a scheme shows the Spanish military genius at its height, and represents a feat of seamanship and discipline which had never been attempted at sea before, and has scarcely ever been achieved again. Even in fine weather, to form this huge and disparate fleet of ships into a precise formation, and to preserve it in the face of repeated attacks, was an extraordinary achievement. Certainly the English, who as yet had no practice in fleet manoeuvres, could not have achieved anything of the kind. No English fleet of merchantmen and warships in company attempted to sail in

IX.   *The Fire Ship Attack, 7 August.*

precise formation in the face of the enemy before the eighteenth century, and nothing as exact as the Spanish order seems to have been attained before the twentieth century brought steamships and signalling to make it possible. For Howard and his admirals the sight of Spanish discipline at sea must have been a very unpleasant shock. They faced a completely new and unexpected problem, for if the Spanish formation was not broken there could be no hope of victory. For the next week they were to make repeated, gallant and futile attempts to do so.

On that first morning each side went into battle with the gestures of the traditions of chivalry: Medina Sidonia hoisted his sacred banner to the maintop, and Howard sent his pinnace the *Disdain* to bear his challenge to the Spanish admiral, like a herald sent forth from a mediaeval army. Then he led the English ships to attack the northern, shoreward wing of the Spanish fleet. At the same time another group of ships led by Drake, Hawkins and Frobisher attacked the other wing. On both flanks the Spaniards attempted to lure the English to close action, and on the seaward Martinez de Recalde the commander of that squadron allowed himself to be cut off from his colleagues in the hope of provoking a boarding action, but the English refused to be drawn. They subjected the Spanish ships to the heaviest fire possible from a safe range, but always kept well out of reach. When the Spaniards attempted to attack, the English ships kept their distance with derisory ease.

So the first day ended, unsatisfactory to both sides. The Spaniards had suffered the frustration of being attacked with little prospect of retaliation. Moreover it was becoming clear that their intelligence had been wrong, and the squadron which had come out of Plymouth was the main body of the English fleet and not a detachment. Expecting to meet the principal English force ahead and to leeward, Medina Sidonia had put his best fighting ships ahead of the convoy rather than in the two wings astern which were bearing the English attack. For the English affairs seemed much worse. A regular attack with the whole fleet had apparently done nothing to break Spanish formation. Moreover the English ships, which had put to sea with at most thirty rounds of ammunition a gun, had by then expended much of it, and urgent appeals for powder and shot were dispatched ashore. So great a cannonade had never been seen before; to find it ineffective was deeply worrying.

After this day's fighting the Spaniards suffered by accident their only serious losses. The *Nuestra Senora del Rosario,* flagship of the Andalusian Squadron, lost her bowsprit in a collision, and the *San Salvador,* vice-flagship of the Guipuzcoan Squadron, was badly damaged by a powder explosion. Soon afterwards the *Rosario's* foremast went overboard, and having failed in an attempt to tow her, Medina Sidonia was obliged to leave her in the darkness.

Meanwhile in the English fleet Howard had disposed his ships for the night, ordering them to keep station on the stern lantern of Drake's flagship the *Revenge.* Sometime during the night the fleet lost sight of that lantern, and in the morning the Lord Admiral found himself close astern of the Spaniards but without almost all his own fleet. Sir Francis, meanwhile, had taken possession of the *Rosario,* and neither he nor the rest of the fleet rejoined Howard until the afternoon. Howard was too magnanimous a commander for recriminations at a moment when unity was so important, and Drake's admirers have laboured subsequently to explain his night's work in a favourable light, but it is hard to avoid the suspicion that the instincts of a lifetime of piracy had overcome him. The character of a respectable admiral sat lightly on almost all the great Elizabethan seamen, perhaps most lightly of all on Drake. It looks very much as though he put out his stern lantern in order to take the rich prize which suddenly offered. The result was to put the Lord Admiral in imminent danger, and at best to lose the chance of effective action at the very moment when the Spaniards, had they been contemplating a landing, might have hauled up for Torbay. But naval strategy scarcely existed, all the English commanders had been brought up to regard a rich prize as the highest object of warfare at sea, and it seems that no-one blamed Drake. At least the English had gained their first success, and gained it, against all probability, without a fight, for Pedro de Valdes made little attempt to repair his ship and none at all to defend her. Later that day the English gained their second prize, the abandoned and waterlogged wreck of the *San Salvador.* Otherwise there was no fighting, and the Spaniards employed the day in reorganising their formation, shifting many of the best galleons from the van to the two wings which had borne almost all of the fighting.

The following morning, which was Tuesday, both fleets were off Portland Bill, and the wind came from the south-eastward, giving the Spaniards again the weather-gage. Throughout the morning the English ships attempted to beat around the Armada's flanks to regain it, while the Spaniards attempted to prevent them and force a close action. In the first object they succeeded, but in spite of heavy firing on both sides, the English still kept their distance and avoided any risk of boarding. During a day of heavy and confused fighting the wind shifted back to the westward, and by nightfall the two fleets were in much the same position as before: the Armada creeping ponderously eastward, the English dogging its heels. Once more the English ships had expended a prodigious quantity of powder and shot and Howard's anguished pleas for fresh supplies were redoubled. Once more they had completely failed to break the Spanish formation. The two ships taken had both been crippled by accidents, and if, as the English were sure, several Spanish ships had been severely handled, it did not seem to have had any effect on the cohesion of the Armada as a whole. For real victory it was essential to break that formidable order, and the English were no nearer breaking it.

For the next three days, from Wednesday to Friday, the two fleets moved slowly up Channel before very light breezes. The Spaniards held to their purpose of meeting Parma, to whom a stream of messages was despatched, warning him to be ready to embark as

X.	*The Battle of Gravelines, 8 August.*

soon as the Armada appeared. The English concentrated on preventing the most immediate peril, a landing on the South Coast. Both sides seized every chance of action, but neither was able to bring on a decisive battle. On Wednesday morning the English surrounded a Spanish straggler, the *Gran Griffon,* and fought a hot action with the Spanish ships which came to relieve her. That afternoon the wind fell away completely, and Howard took the opportunity to hold a council of war which addressed the question of tactics. The previous day the English fleet had split into at least three unco-ordinated parts, while once again the Spaniards had been saved from serious damage by their unity and discipline. Beyond what seems to have been a general custom of attacking in something like line ahead to deploy their broadside guns to best advantage, the English captains had shown themselves innocent of tactics or fleet organisation. The contrast with the Spanish performance was glaring, and that afternoon it was decided to break up the English fleet into four squadrons, commanded by Howard, Drake, Hawkins and Martin Frobisher, the well-known Arctic explorer. The new organisation does not seem to have extended to any sort of formation beyond the line ahead, or any but the most informal co-ordination between the squadrons, but at least it gave some prospect that the ships might be handled more effectively than was possible with a fleet of nearly a hundred sail in a body.

The next morning, being Thursday, the two fleets were off the Isle of Wight, and in light airs, part of the day almost flat calm, there was further confused fighting. The moment was, or might have been, critical, for the Spaniards had already identified the Isle of Wight as their best prospect of a landing on the South Coast, and if they could enter Spithead with their formidable discipline intact it might have been extremely difficult for the English to have dislodged them. At the time when they would have had to haul up for the anchorage, Drake's squadron was pressing hard on the seaward wing of the Armada and tending to drive it further eastward and inshore. Whether this was deliberate or not, it forced the Spaniards towards the Owers, the shoals which stretch out from Selsey Bill and form the eastern perimeter of the broad entrance to Spithead. It was essential for Medina Sidonia and his admirals to make a quick decision; either to haul up close and commit themselves to trying to get into Spithead, there to land their troops in the presence of the English fleet and establish a bridgehead on the island, or to alter course to seaward, follow their orders and continue down the Channel to where the Duke of Parma awaited them with his invincible army. Disobedience might possibly have gained a famous victory, but it would have been extremely risky to have attempted a landing with an undefeated fleet at their back, and neither Medina Sidonia's character nor his orders encouraged recklessness. The Armada stood away south-easterly, leaving the Isle of Wight and the English coast behind them.

For the English this was something like a victory at last. The Spaniards were still undefeated, but at least Howard had managed 'so to course the enemy as that they shall have no leisure to land'. On Friday morning he knighted Hawkins, Frobisher and several of his captains on his quarter-deck. But though they had something to celebrate, the situation remained very grave. There was now no hope of preventing Medina Sidonia's junction with the Duke of Parma. The greatest fleet would be joined to the finest army in the world, and if the English navy could not defeat the former, it was hardly to be hoped that the improvised English army could face the latter. Only the difficulties of geography which the Spaniards would have to overcome, and the powerful reinforcement of Lord Henry Seymour's squadron waiting in the Straits of Dover, gave the English any confidence.

For the Spaniards the crisis of the campaign was approaching. Undefeated and undaunted, they now approached the decisive rendezvous with Parma's army, the object towards which King Philip's orders directed them with such finality. How Parma would or could pass the obstacles which divided him from Medina Sidonia was a question to which the Duke urgently needed an answer. None of his despatches had returned from Parma, the weather was breaking up, and the Armada could go no further without hearing from him.

So on Saturday evening, (27th July by the English reckoning) the Spaniards, disciplined as ever, anchored in formation off the French port of Calais, and the English anchored just to windward of them. Late that evening Seymour's squadron from the Downs joined the English fleet, bringing it to its greatest strength of about 140 sail.

It was predictable that the Spaniards would have to anchor somewhere if they were to make rendezvous with Parma, and it was equally obvious what to do about it. Orders had been given some days before to prepare fireships, but they had not joined the English fleet by the Sunday morning when Howard once more summoned his council of war. Something had to be done at once; the Armada was only thirty miles from Parma at Dunkirk, and the governor of Calais, nominally neutral, was believed to be an adherent of the Catholic League and consequently friendly to Spain. Whether he came overland or by water, Parma would doubtless come soon, and the Armada had to be driven off first. The English decided not to wait for the arrival of the intended fireships, but at once to improvise them from some of the smaller ships of the fleet. Drake and Hawkins each offered a ship of their own, others were found, and that Sunday night, with the wind freshening and the spring tide assisting, they were loosed on the Spanish ships.

Medina Sidonia had foreseen and provided for just such an attack. A screen of pinnaces was in position to grapple and tow off the fireships, and if any should nevertheless get through, the Spanish ships had orders to slip and buoy their cables, to haul off to seaward only so far as was essential to avoid the fireships, and to be ready to return to their anchorage in the morning. Unfortunately the memory of the explosive fireships used by the Dutch at Antwerp, which had nearly killed the great Duke of Parma himself and whose inventor was known to be in England, was fresh in the Spanish fleet. For the first and last time, when the fireships bore down the Spaniards panicked and the discipline of the

Map of the Kent Beacons. W. Lambarde. Ad. ms. 62935. By permission of the British Library.

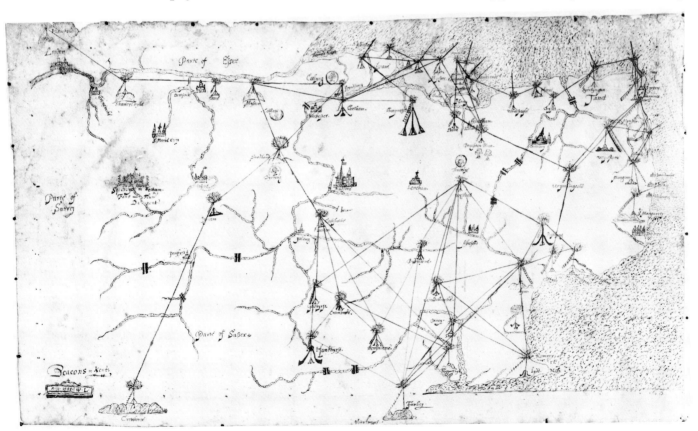

Armada disintegrated. Two of the fireships were grappled and towed aside; six swept down on the achorage. Medina Sidonia and four other galleons only followed his orders; the rest cut their cables and fled in a disorderly mob towards the Zealand Banks. Not one was actually burnt by the fireships, but they had nevertheless gained what the English had never yet achieved; they had broken the formidable Spanish formation.

At dawn the English saw what they had done, and at once they weighed anchor to attack. Only Medina Sidonia's five galleons were in sight, plus one damaged galleass inshore. This ship the Lord Admiral took for himself, leaving the other four divisions of his fleet to attack the galleons. This was a mistake, which undoubtedly he would never had made had he known that he was missing the Spanish admiral, for the boarding and looting of the galleass, driven ashore under the guns of Calais, wasted several hours and prevented Howard rejoining the main action until the afternoon. Meanwhile the other English ships had at last an open battle, a fleeing enemy among whom they could pick their targets. Medina Sidonia stubbornly fought a rearguard action, giving time for his scattered ships to rejoin him, but with its formidable discipline, and most of its ammunition, gone, the Armada began to suffer severely for the first time. It seems that the English realised that they would have to close the range to achieve results, and with the Spanish formation

The Armada's Progress from Plymouth to Gravelines. Claes Jansz Visscher, pre-1615. NMM. 70 I 1588.

a. The Battle of Portland.

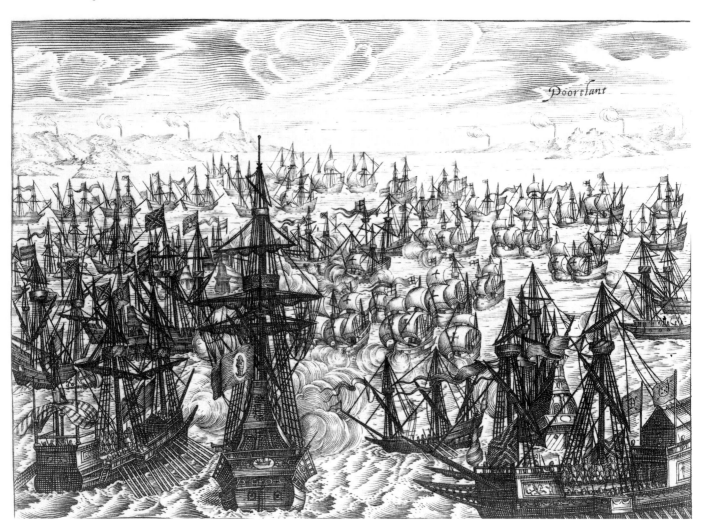

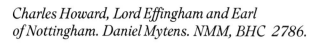
Charles Howard, Lord Effingham and Earl of Nottingham. Daniel Mytens. NMM, BHC 2786.

Sir Francis Drake. Nicholas Hilliard, c.1540-1596. NPG 4851. Reproduced by permission of the National Portrait Gallery.

*Portrait of Don Alvaro de Bazan, primer Marques de Santa Cruz. Spanish School.
Reproduced by permission of La Marquesa de Santa Cruz.*

*Queen Elizabeth I: the Armada Portrait. English School. Reproduced by permission of
William Tyrwhitt-Drake Esq.*

The Armada in the Strait of Dover. Flemish School, c.1600-1610. NMM PR 82/17.

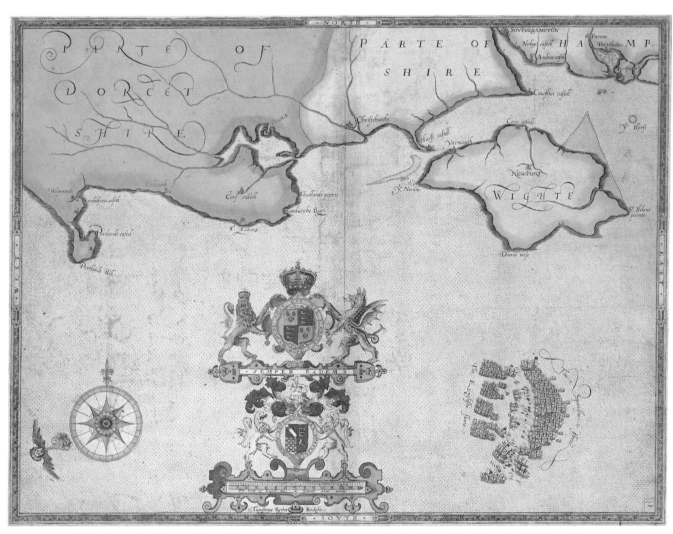

The Armada Charts from 'Expeditiones Hispanorum in Angliam Vera Descriptio Anno Do.:
MDLXXXVIII.' No. 7, The Battle off the Isle of Wight, 4 August. Augustine Ryther after Robert Adams, 1590. NMM.

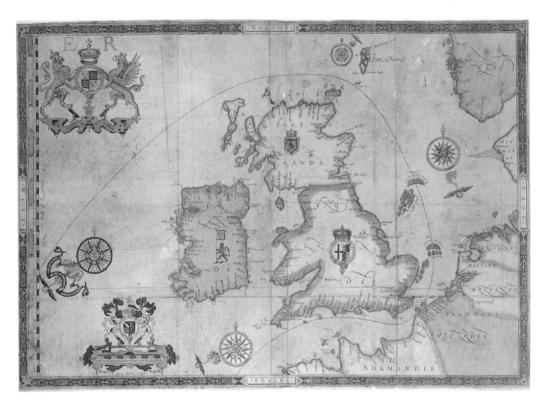

Chart showing the track of the Armada. Augustine Ryther after Robert Adams, 1590. NMM. G218:1/8.

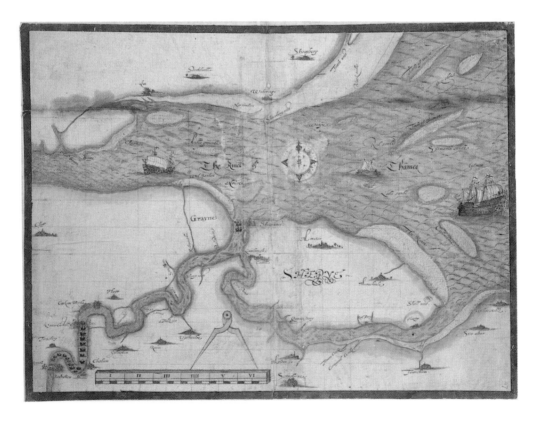

Chart of the Medway and the Mouth of the Thames. Pen, pencil and colour wash, c.1580. Hatfield House. Reproduced by permission of the Marquess of Salisbury.

broken up they were at last able to do so. Moreover the weather was worsening, with rising winds and falling visibility. In spite of all that weather and gunfire could do, however, the discipline of the Spanish fleet and the dauntless courage of their commander gradually reconstructed their formation, so that by afternoon the English once more faced a regular line of fighting ships. But at really close range, with many Spanish ships completely out of round shot and replying only with small arms, the English were able for the first time to inflict serious damage. At least two Spanish ships were sunk, and two more drove on the shoals and were taken by the Dutch. All the while the wind was driving the two fleets towards the Zealand banks - and there was no doubt which of the two would be able to claw off to windward.

All through the night the English followed the Spaniards as they drove into shoal water, waiting for their inevitable destruction. From this peril the battered Spanish fleet was saved, as they believed, by a miracle. At the last possible moment, soon after dawn on the Tuesday, the wind shifted suddenly to the southward, allowing the Spaniards to haul off to the northwards and once more restore their formation. By this time the English too were almost out of ammunition, and could not renew the action. So the two fleets sailed north-eastwards into the North Sea, the English, as they put it, 'putting on a brag countenance' and hoping that their bluff would not be called before they received fresh powder and shot. No one believed that the fighting was over. The English resolved to watch the Spanish fleet until it was certain that they would not land in England or Scotland.

b. Inscribed Dunne Nose (St. Catherine's Point, Isle of Wight).

For their part the Spaniards were in a difficult if not desperate position. Short of food, water and ammunition, with many ships badly damaged, they were in no condition for a long voyage, but they had no hope of returning to southward and resuming their mission unless the wind shifted. Damaged as they were, they could not hope to beat against the wind. Given the chance they resolved to renew the fight with what means they had, make contact with Parma if God should make it possible, and somehow complete their task. If the wind should hold there was nothing to do but attempt to return by a voyage north-about Scotland and so home to Spain - a voyage for which they were in no condition. Although the English feared the Armada would take refuge in a Danish or Norwegian port, no diplomatic contacts or preparations had been made to do so, and Medina Sidonia rejected the possibility. Meanwhile the south-westerly wind held. On 2nd August by their reckoning, past the latitude of the Forth, the English turned away in search of victuals and ammunition, leaving the Spaniards to hold on northwards.

Though no-one realised it, this was the last time the two main fleets were to be in contact, and the last contribution of the English fleet to the campaign. Pinnaces continued to follow the Spaniards until they were past Fair Isle and it was quite clear that they were bound for Spain, but the English main fleet returned to the Thames in search of ammunition, victuals, and fresh men to replace those who were dying more and more rapidly. As it became clear that the threat had passed, the fleet was laid up: food, money and powder were virtually exhausted, the men sickened and died in thousands, but their task was done. Before any Spaniards had reached Spain, most of Queen Elizabeth's ships were once more lying to their buoys in the Medway.

Meanwhile the Spanish Armada faced the long voyage home. Few of the ships had victuals or water sufficient for such a passage. Many of them were badly damaged, with heavy casualties. Exhausted by days of fighting, demoralized by the consciousness of defeat, they struggled westward into the autumn gales of the North Atlantic. Medina Sidonia was as always calm and resolute. His orders were to keep company and not to turn southward for Spain until the ships had reached far out into the Atlantic, 'and to take great heed lest you fall upon the island of Ireland'. All those who kept his orders the Duke brought home to Spain; sixty-seven sail in all, including most of the best galleons. The ships were nearly all damaged, some very badly; many men were dead or near death from disease and thirst, and they continued to die for weeks after the ships made port. Two of Spain's most experienced admirals, Juan Martinez de Recalde and Miguel de Oquendo, died within weeks of returning to Spain.

The ships which parted company from the Duke were nearly all lost at sea or wrecked, mostly on the west coast of Ireland, and only a handful of survivors ever reached home, via neutral Scotland. Several thousands were killed by the English and Irish; one or two may perhaps have survived to settle among the people they regarded as savages, but there can be no truth in the legend of a 'Spanish' physical type common in Connaught and Mayo, inherited from survivors of the Armada. Those who survived were those Medina Sidonia brought home to Spain, and to him belongs the credit, not only for an epic voyage in the face of appalling adversity, but for making the best that any man could of King Philip's orders. Perhaps a more charismatic figure than the duke might have inspired greater loyalty among his followers, or greater sympathy among historians, but it is hard to see that any one could have done more than he did.

The Armada failed because the preparation of an adequate fleet, with sufficient stores and armament, was beyond the administrative resources even of Spain, and though England was far weaker than Spain, the English fleet was in all material respects the stronger. Whatever hope the Armada might have had of success was eliminated by King Philip's impossible strategy. Perhaps if the English had made some serious mistake, such as accepting a close action on Spanish terms, and if Medina Sidonia had been prepared to abandon his orders and boldly exploit the opportunity, the Armada might have triumphed,

24

but the odds against it were high. For a sea-borne invasion to have a real hope of success Philip needed to devote many years of money and effort to preparing the ground: in Flanders, by capturing Flushing and building up naval strength; in Spain, by establishing a standing navy with a permanent administration capable of sustaining a great fleet. Efforts were made in both directions, but as always Spanish resources were spread too thinly, Spain fought on too many fronts, and the necessary conditions for the invasion of England were never established. In later years two further Armadas sailed for the conquest of England, but with no more success than the first. Philip envisaged the invasion of England in 1588 as the decisive stroke which would overcome all his difficulties, but in truth it was only likely to have succeeded after he had overcome elsewhere and could turn all his resources to the formidable problems of invasion by sea. Perhaps no sixteenth-century state, even one as rich and powerful as Spain, could ever have overcome the obstacles of geography and the skilful defence of the English.

Documents

1   THE PRICE OF ADMIRALTY

The last page of a detailed mobilization scheme drawn up in 1580: to send the Queen's ships and twenty-two selected merchant ships to sea for three months would cost about 15 per cent of the gross annual revenues of the English Crown.

Ann Abstracte, or Substaunce, of this book

    Whatt the great warraunt must include

ffirste for the Chardge of thre monnethes, for all her ma[jest]is shippes	[£]24996-1[s]-8[d]
Secondly the Chardge of 32[1] marchanntes shippes	[£]28000-0[s]-0[d]
Thirdly the Chardge of Cordaige and Canvis	[£]03000-0[s]-0[d]
So as the whole warraunt must bee	[£]45996-1[s]-8[d]

    What Chardge must Issew out of the greatt warrannt if the shippes stand in order w[i]th ther smale nombres[2] thre monnethes

ffirst for her ma[jes]tis owne shippes for three monnet[h]s Chardge	[£]10564-16[s]-6[d]
Secondly for xxij marchannts shippes	[£]05284-0[s]-0[d]
Thirdly for p[ro]vition of Cordaige & Canvis	[£]03000-0[s]-0[d]
Totalls	[£]18851-16[s]-6[d]

State Papers Domestic, 1580, SP 12/143 No.20, f. 60v

1   Actually 22, as below.

2   i.e. with reduced crews.

An Abstracte, or Subsstaunce, of this book

Wsatt the great warraunt most motued

Firste for the charge of this monethes, for all hir maiesties shippes ———————— 24996 — 1 — 8

Secondly the charge of 32 marrchauntes shippes ——————————————— 18000 — 0 — 0

Thirdly the charge of cordage and cantvis ———————————————— 03000 — 0 — 0

So the wholle warraunt most then bee ——— 45996 — 1 — 8

That charge most Issue out of the greatt warraunt if the shippes stand in orde & wth the small nomber this monethes

First for hir maiesties owne shippes for theire monethes charge ———————— 10567 — 16 — 6

Secondly for own marrchantes shippes — 05284 — 0 — 0

Thirdly for addition of cordage & cantvis 03000 — 0 — 0

Totall ———— 18851 — 16 — 6

2 PRIVATISING THE DOCKYARDS

The terms of the contract under which Hawkins, as a private contractor, undertook the annual maintenance of the Navy. This is apparently the original contract of 1579, annotated by Burghley in 1588 when its success, and renewal, were being considered.

The Bargayne of John Hawkins for the Navye, Viz:

Condic[i]ons in the behalfe of her ma[jes]tie

1   ffirst all that w[hi]ch was ordinary in such tyme as it was v^m vii^c xiiii li[1] yerelie John Hawkins shall p[er]forme

2   As first to pay and contynewe the same number of Shippe keep[er]s that hath bene since the saide ordinarie was reduced to the saide Some of 5714 li together w[i]th the same nomber of gonne[r]s in Upnor Castle[2] the Clerkes &c. the Watchemen and Rent that nowe is paied in the ordinarye.

3   It[e]m to kepe in repayer all hir ma[jes]ties Shippes so as uppon A groundinge they may be readie to s[er]ve at the Seas[3] untill some one of them come to be newe made in A drie docque.

4   It[e]m to moare the Navye sufficientlie so that the Shippes maye ride w[i]thout daunger.

5   It[e]m to repayer all manner of Storehouses and wharfes at Chatham Wolwich, Deptford and Portesmouth untill any of them shall fall into such decayie as they must be newe built.

6   It[e]m to contynewe all hir ma[jes]ties Navye in s[er]viceable order and everie yere to doe such rep[er]ac[i]ons as shalbe nedefull either in makinge of A newe Shippe repayringe in drie docques or any way otherwyse that shalbe nedeful so that the full nomber be kept as they are nowe at this p[re]sent yf any S[h]ippe be decayed an nother to be put newe in the place of like leng[t]h and breadth sufficiently builded. [marginal note in Burghley's hand: 'non at all war made new by hy[m]']

7   It[e]m to grounde the Shippes uppon all occasions of Sea s[er]vice Leakes or other nedefull causes.

8   It[e]m all the Boates Cocks, Pynnasses and Lyghters shalbe kept in s[er]viceable order, and as the olde doe decaye newe to be made in their places.

9   It[e]m he shall finde Norwaye mastes for all the smalle Shippes under the Ayde[4] and the Toppe mastes and toppe Sayle yardes of all the Shippes.

10   It[e]m that at all hallowtide[5] everie yere there shalbe presented unto the Lorde Treasourer, the Lorde Chamb[er]layne, Mr Secretarye and Sir Walter mildmay the names of twentie skillfull men as Captaynes, Gonners, Shipwrights and masters of w[hi]ch number the foresaide Com[m]ission[er]s shall appoynt such A nomber as they will to make report of the estate of the Navye, and to showe their opynion what shalbe nedefull to be donne to the Navye and yere followinge w[hi]ch shalbe likewise p[er]formed.

State Papers Domestic, 1588, SP 12/208 No.17, ff. 45v-46r

1   i.e. £5714, as below.
2   The battery defending the Medway achorage.
3   Ships went into dry dock only for major rebuilding; for small repairs and cleaning their bottoms they were grounded to be worked on at low water.
4   i.e. smaller than the *Aid* of 250 tons.
5   The feast of All Hallows is 1st November.

Condic[i]ons in the behalfe of John Hawkins.

1 ffirst the saide John Hawkins shall have paied hym for the s[e]rvice to be donne of thother side[6] the olde ordinarie Warraunt of 5714 li-2s-2d monethlie as it was in Anno 1578,

2 It[e]m he shalbe holpen w[i]th the Com[m]ission as in Anno 1578.

3 It[e]m it shalbe Lawfull for hym to entertayne as many Shipwrightes as he will and as fewe as he will and at all seasons and tymes as the s[er]vice shall require and noe more.

4 yf any of the Shippes shall come to A mischaunce (as god forbidde) either by fier, wracke, spoyle in warre or such like or the Boates Cocks or Pynnasses then the saide John Hawkins shall have allowaunce for the supplie of such Shippes Boates and Pynnasses as the Chardge shall require and be iudged by the Com[m]ission[er]s or officers of the Navie.

5 It[e]m that yf the hole Navye shall goe to the Seas or A greate p[ar]te of them whatsoever provisions of tymber Borde and Plancke shalbe taken into them for Sea s[e]rvice, the saide John Hawkins shall not be Chardged w[i]th above the value of xls. in such stuffe for everie Shippe to Saye Boardes, Plancke, ffysshers for mastes Spare mastes for Toppe mastes and such like.

6 It[e]m the saide John Hawkins shall have the Assistaunce of the Shippe keap[er]s for the helpe of groundinge of the Shippes Loadinge and unloadinge of provisions and such like, the use of the Whoy for Cariadge Launtchinge, tackles, and Crane Roopes &c as hath bene in tyme past.

7 It[e]m he shall also have the use of the Wharfes, Storehouses, fforges and Lodgings at Chatham, Deptforde, Wolwich and Portsmouth for those ministers that shalbe nedefull to attende this s[er]vice, and for the Layinge of all manner of p[ro]visions readilie for the saide s[e]rvice.

8 It[e]m that yf the Shippes shall ride in any other place by hir ma[jes]ties order then by the discrec[i]on of the Com[m]ission[er]s it maye be iudged what shalbe increased for the same moaringe, callinge unto them Thofficers and masters of the Navye.[7]

9 It[e]m that when A newe Shippe shalbe made and readie to be Launtched the saide John Hawkins shall make his Comoditie of Tholde.[8]

10. It[e]m yf any ambiguitie or doubt shall happen of either p[ar]te that ought to be Considered in equitie and Conscience, be omitted in this bargayne and that the same can not be agreed uppon amongst the officers, that then the Com[m]ission[er]s aforesaide shall by their discrec[i]ons moderate the doubt and order the same.

6 The 'conditions in the behalf of her Majesty' on the other side.
7 The Officers of the Navy are the members of the Navy Board.
8 Hawkins was entitled to the remains of an old ship replaced.

Demaunde in the behalfe of his maiestie   30 Burgayne

ffirst all that is now ordinary in such sorte as it now is that
yonder John Hawkins shall performe

2   As first to pay and contynewe the same number of shippe keeps
that hath bene since the said ordinarie was reduced to the said somme
of 5714li togeather with the same number of gunners in dyvers castell the
clarkes &c, the waltermen and rent that now is paid in the ordinarie

3   Item to kepe in repayre all his maiesties shippes that upon A grounding
they may be readie to serve at the seas untill some one of them come to be
new made in A drie docque

4   Item to moore the navye sufficientlie so that the shippes maye ride
without dannger

5   Item to repayre all manner of store houses and wharfes at Chatham
Woolwich, deptford, and portesmouth untill any of them shall fall into
such decaye as they must be newe built

6   Item to contynewe all his maiesties navye in serviceable order and everie
yere to doo such reparacons as shalbe needefull either in makinge of
non at all was   A newe shippe repayringe in drie docque or any way otherwise that
made new by   shalbe needefull so that the full number be kept as they are now at
his   this present of any shippe be decayed an other to be put newe in her
place of like lenght and breadth sufficientlie builded

7   Item to grounde the shippes upon all occasions of sea fights
leakes or other needefull causes

8   Item all the boates yorke barrgges and lyghters shalbe kept
in serviceable order, and as the olde doo decaye newe to be made in
their places

9   Item he shall finde Norway masts for all the smalle shippes
under the Ada and the toppe masts and toppe gaste yardes of
all the shippes

10   Item that at all hallontide everie yere there shalbe presented
unto the Lorde Treasurer, the Lorde Chamblayne, mr Controuler
and Sr Walter Rawley the names of twentie skilfull men as
captaynes gonners shipwrightes and masters of which number the
foresaid commissioners shall appoynt such A number as they will to
make report of the estate of the navye, and to shewe there
oppinion what shalbe needefull to be done to the navye the yere
followinge which shalbe likewise performed

of John Hawkins for the Navye Docke

Condicions in the behalfe of John Hawkins.

1. First the said John Hawkins shall have paied him for the care to be donne of the shipp the other ordinarie decrement of / 5714 / 2 / in monthlie as it arose in Anno 1578

2. Item he shallbe holpen with the daire as in Anno 1578

3. Item it shallbe lawfull for him to enterteyne as many shipwrightes as he will and as fewe as he will and at all seasons and tymes as the shipp shall require and no more

4. If any of the shippes shall come to a mischance as god forbidd either by fier, wracke, storme in waves or suche like or the Boates Docke or Wharffes then the said John Hawkins shall have allowance for the supplie of suche shippes Boates and wharffes as the chardge shall require and be indged by the Commissiond or officers of the navye

5. Item that of the said navye shall goe to the seas or otherwise yf the of them whatsoever provision of tymber Borde and plancke shallbe taken into them for care there, the said John Hawkins shall not be chardged with above the value of [deleted] in suche stuffe for everie shipp to carye Boardes, plancke, timbers for masts Spanne mastes for toppe mastes and suche like.

6. Item the said John Hawkins shall have the assistance of the Shippe keeps for the helpe of groundige of the shippes loadinge and unloadinge of provisions and suche like, the use of the hoyes for carriage, launchinge, carkes and screwe ropes &c. as hath bene in tyme past

7. Item he shall also have the use of the wharfes, storehowse, howses and lodgings at Chatham, Deptforde, Wolwich and Portesmouth for those ministers that shallbe nedefull to attende this service, and for the layinge of all manner of provisions neadefull for the said service.

8. Item that if the shippes shall ride in any other place by his matis order then by the appointmen of the Commissiond it maye be indged right and meatood of the navye.

9. Item that when a newe shippe shalbe made and readie to be launched the said John Hawkins shall make his demandes of the same.

10. Item yf any ambiguitie or doubt shall happen of either side that ought to be considered in equitie and conscience, be omitted in this language and that the same can not be agreed upon amongst the officers, then the Commissiond aforesaid shall by their discretions moderate the doubt and order the same.

3   SINGEING THE KING OF SPAIN'S BEARD

In his inimitably vigorous but obscure style, and his own appalling handwriting, Drake reports to Sir Francis Walsingham the proceedings of his squadron on the coast of Portugal.

Since the dep|ar|ting of captayne crosse, Right honorable, ther hathe happened, betwene the spanyards, Portyngalles & our selves, dyvers combatts, in the wh|ich| it hathe pleased god that we have taken, fortts, shipes, barks, carvelles and dyvers other vesselles, more than a hundreth most laden, sum w|it|h oorse for gallyes, plancks and tymber, for shippes and penaces, howpes and pype staves, for casks, w|it|h many other provytyons for this great armey, I a suer yor ho|nour| the howpes and pype staves, were a bove 16 or 17 C tonn in wayght, wh|ich| cannott be lesse then 25 or 30 thowsand tonn if it had byn mad in caske redy for lyqwyer[1], all wh|ich| I comaunded to be consumed into smoke and asshes by fier, wh|ich| wilbe unto the K|ing| no small want of his provycyons, besyde the want of his barks. the netts wh|ich| we have consumed will cawse the people to carse ther governours to ther ffaces......

[two paragraphs omitted]

In the revenge of these thinges, what forces the contry is abell to make, we shalbe suer to have brought uppon us as ffarr, as the|y| may, w|it|h all the devyces and trappes the|y| cann devyse, I thancke them mych, the|y| have stayed so long, & when they com, they shalbe but the sunes of morttall men & for the most part, enemyes to the truthe, & upholders of balles or dagones Image[2], wh|ich| hath alredye ffallen beforr the arke of our god w|it|h his, hands, armes, and head stroken of. aslong as it shall please god to geve us provycyons to eat and drincke, and that our shipes, & wynd and wether will p|er|mett us, yo shall surly hyer of us nerre this cape of St.Vencent, wher we doe and will expect daylly what her ma|jes|t|y| and yor honors will farther comaund.

god make us all thankffull that her ma|jes|ti sent out these ffewe shipes in tyme,

yf ther were her vj more of her ma|jes|tes good shippes, of the Second sort[3], we should be the better abell to kepe ther forces from Joynyng, and happelly take or impeache his fletts from all places, in the next monthe and so after wh|ich| is the chefest tymes of ther returnes home[4] wh|ich| I Judge in my powr opynyon, will bring this great monarchy to those condycyons wh|ich| ar meett,

Ther most be a begynnyng of any great matter, but the contenewing, unto thend untyll itt be thouroghly ffynyshed yldes the trew glory yf hanyball had ffollowed his victoryes. it is thowght of many. he had never bynn taken by Sepyo[5], god mak us all thankffull agayne, and agayne that we have althowgh it be letell mad a begenyng upon the cost of Spayne, yf we can throwghly beleve, that this wh|ich| we doe is in the defenc of our relygyon, and contrye, no Doubt but our mercyffull god, for his christ, our Savyours Sake, is abell and will geve us victory although our sennes be reed, god geve us grace, we may feare hym, & daylly to call upon hym, So shall nether Sattan, nor his menesters prevyell agaynst us, althowgh god permeett Job to be toucht in body, yeat the lord will hold his mynd pure, Lett me be pardoned of y|ou|r ho|nour| agayne & agayne for my over myche boldnes, it is the conffecyon, or my owne concyence, my dutty in all humbellnes to y|ou|r ho|nour| my good lady y|ou|r yocke p|ar|tner and all yors, beseching yo all to pray unto god hartelly for us, as we doe daylly for all yors, beseching yo all to pray unto god hartelly for us, as we doe daylly for all you, hast from her ma|jes|tes good shipe the Ellyzabeth bonaventure now ryding at cape Sake[6] this 17 may 1587

y|ou|r ho|nour's| most redy to be comanded

Fra: Drake

State Papers Domestic 1588, SP 12/201 No.33, ff. 71-72

1   The English tun generally held 252 gallons: Drake is claiming to have destroyed the capacity of six or seven million gallons.

2   Baal's or Dagon's image: cf. II Kings 10:27 and I Samuel 5:2-4.

3   The 'middling sort'; the newest design of galleon.

4   The return home of the treasure fleets from the Caribbean.

5   Drake was not perfectly familiar with the careers of Hannibal and Scipio.

6   Cape Sagres.

Some the doynge of rasinge... [illegible] ... ther late happened, betwene the spaynard, portugalls ... [illegible] ... other combatte, in the w[hi]ch it hathe pleased god that we have taken, fortt, shippes, bark [illegible] ... and other vessells, more then a hundreth most laden, som w[i]th coorn for gallyes, plankes and tymber, for shipes and ... powder and ... [illegible] ... for raffe, w[i]th many other ... for this great armey. ... a fewer yere ... the ... and these ... were a boute 16 or 17 ... in ... w[hi]ch ... cannott be leffe then 25 or 30 thousand tonn of it had ... made in ... w[i]th for expence, all w[hi]ch ... remaineth to be consumed into smoke and asshes by fier, w[hi]ch will breede no small want of ... prouisions, to suple the want of these boate the moste w[i]th we have consumed will cause the people to ... them ... to ther slaue.

the portugalls I have allwayes comaunded to be usid well, and sett them at ... w[i]th owt ... of any ther appar... and have made them to knowe that it was vnto me agreable ... that I was order the ... of theft to the bellow of over... off ... but that I found them imployed for the ... Spayn and Spaynisse w[hi]ch are told to be owr mortall enemyes, and take som portugalls so ... now in ther ... and put them a land in ... other places, neuer w[i]th ... off we ... owr ... the rom ... will be ... all ... and they as ... for sure ... mafter, rather then to be sold as slaves. ... a som ... this ... breed a great ... in the spaynard ... the marchyse of Sarinse at last ... men Lysbona, by messinger, w[he]ther he was a ... the gallyes, to knowe w[he]ther he would vedeme any of this... w[hi]ch I tould som ... for off, for suche of my mastyes people as are ...

4   MAINTAINING THE QUEEN'S SHIPS

William Hawkins, Mayor of Plymouth and the Treasurer's brother, reports his work on the small squadron based at Plymouth over the winter of 1588. These were almost the only ships then in commisison.

I have received of Anthony goddard of Plymouth merchant the some of twentie and feive poundes of Corrant mony of England, I saie 25 li., which is to be paide him, or to the bringer hereof in London, at sighte of this bill, by the handes of the righte worship[fu]ll, John Hawkins esquire treasurer of her ma[jes]ties navie, Dated in Plymouth the 17th of februarie 1587.[1]

Your lovyng brother
Wm Hawkyns

the hope & nonp[ar]ylya[2], ar bothe gravyd, tallowyd, & this tyd in to the Rode agayne, and the Revaunge, nowe aground I hope she shall lyckewyse, go into the Rode also to morow we have and dowe trym one syd of every shype, by nyght & the other syd by day, so that, we end the 3 great shypes, in 3 dayes this sprynge[3], the shypes syt aground so strongly, & are so staunche, as If they were mad of a holl trea. the doyng of it is very chargabell, for that it is done, by torch lyght & cracseats[4], & in a nextreame, gale of wynd, w[hi]ch consumes pytch, tallo, & fyrsh[5], abundantly. I wrot you fowr dayes past by clayton, who is gone post, yeastir day I R[eceived] your letter, sent w[i]th s[ir] f[rancis] d[rake] & so I tacke my leave this 17th of febrewary 1587 at 7 of the clocke at nyght.

your lovyng brother
Wm Hawkyns

our barrell pytch is all spent 3 days gone, and very scarse to be had heare, If you send 4 or 5 last[6] it wyll searve well for sea stoer, thes hulkes here have none. If they had I wold bye som.

W.H.

State Papers Domestic, 1588, SP 12/208 No. 72, f.162
1   1588 New Style. This paragraph is a bill (the modern equivalent would be a cheque) in payment for the work.
2   The *Nonpareil.*
3   Spring tide.
4   Cressets.
5   Furze, for burning weed off the ships' bottoms.
6   The last of pitch was 12 barrels, each holding 32 gallons.

I have received of Anthony Goddard of Plymouth merchant
the some of twentie and foure poundes of goodd(?) money of
England II saw 25th which is to be paide him or to the bringer
hereof in London at sighte of this bill by the handes of
the righte worshipfull John Hawkins esquire treasurer of
her maties navie Dated in plymouth the 17th of february
1587

your Lovyng brother
Wry Hawkyns

the hope & nonparilia ar bothe grayd(?) tallowyd, & this
tyde in to the rode agayne, and the bonaventure now agrownd
I hope she shall lyke wyse go in to the rode also tomorrow
we have and doe use bryng one syde of above hyr, thy myght
& she over syde by day, so that we end the 3 great
shyppes in 3 dayes this sprynge the shyppes sitt agrownd
so strongly & also so stanche as if they were made
of a foll tree / the doyng of it is very chargable
for that it is donne by force lyght & rrevearchate(?)
& in a westwarne gaell of wynde we consumed
rosen, tallo & pyche abundantly / I wrot you fowre
dayes past by claybrok who is gone post, yesterday
I had your letter, sent wth Mr f. d. & so I take my
leave this 17th of february 1587 at 7 of the clocke
at nyght.

your Lovyng brother
Wry Hawkyns

our barrell pyche is all spent 3 dayes gonne, and
very skarse to be had here / If you send 4. or 5. last
it wyll serve well for hro toer(?) theris enclosed powr
here now / If they paid I wold they knew /

W. H.

(72)

37

5 LORD HOWARD PRAISES HIS SHIPS

Hawkins' rivals accused him of neglecting the maintenance of the Queen's ships: in this letter to Lord Burghley the Lord Admiral unequivocally rejects the charge.

My Ho[nourable] and good lo[rd] I have receved your letter even as I was waynge To goo out. And for the fyrst parte. I am most hartily To gyve your lo[rdship] Thanks for your ho[nour's] favor. I wyll Aknolyg it w[ith] all my love and redy To dow you any sarvys.

for Mr Hawkyns Bargayne he is presently to repayre To The Court. Wher he shalbe best able To Answer in his owne defence. but This much I wyll say To your lo[rdship] I hav byne A bord of every shyp That goeth out w[ith] me and in every plase wher any may krype[1]. and I dow Thank God That they be in the estate They be in And Ther is nevere on of The[m] That knowse what a leke mense. I hav known when A nadmyrall of England hath gone out and 2 shypse in flyt could not say soo. Ther is non That goeth out now but I durst goo to the Ryall de plato[2], in heer and yet the Ma[ry] Rose and The Swallo. be w[ith] me, who weer shyps in the K[ing's] ma[jesty's] her fathers Tym[3] And Therfor I dare presume gratly That Thos that hav byne maid in her ma[jesty's] Tyme be very good and sarvysable. and shall prove The[m] arrant lyers That have reported The Contrary, And I Thank God heer Ma[jesty] I hope may be well Assured of Ther goodnes. yet every Thyng hath his Tyme and must be helped as ned requyrethe.

My lo[rd] I had no menynge To Cary A Way all the offysers[4] I hav non w[ith] me but Sir W.Wynter. I lev Mr Hawkynse and Mr Bowres[5] behynde To wayte on your lo[rdship] and To put The 4 grat shypse in Redynes. wych we shall greatly ned yf The Spanysh forses Come out, and so my lo[rd] havyng no mor lesur To wryght at large being under sayll I bid your lo[rdship] most hirtilie farwell The 22 of Fe[bruary] at 12 A cluk the After noone

your lo[rdship's] most assured To Comand

C. Howard

State Papers Domestic, 1588, SP 12/208 No.79, f. 181, holograph

1 Creep.
2 The Rio de la Plata.
3 Howard was mistaken; these were new ships, not the same as those which had borne their names in Henry VIII's time.
4 The Officers of the Navy, meaning the members of the Navy Board.
5 William Boroughs.

My Ho and good L I have receved your letter eun as I was waynge to
goo out. And for the fyrst parte. I am more hartely to gyue yow L Thankes for
your ho fauor. I wyll Alwayes it fd all my loue and redy to do yow any
servys.

for Mr. Hawkyns Bargayne. he is presently to repayr to the Cowrt wher he
shalbe wel able to Answer in his dewe defense. but this muche I wyll say to
yow L I haue byne A borrd of euery shyppe that goethe out to me and in
euery place wher any may knowe. and I doth Thank God that they be
in the estate they be in And ther is nedara on of the that knoweth what
A leke meaneth. I haue knowen when A nauyroall of England hath gone
out and 2 shyppe in flyt cowd not say soo. Ther is non that goeth out
now but I dare goo to the Ryall de Plato. in heer and yet the Ma.
Rose and the Swallo. be tow me who weer shypps in the K. ma. Tyme
And therfor I haue pesumer gratly that thos they hath byne maued in hir
Ma. Tyme. be uery good and servysable. and shall spede the arrant lyers
that hath reported the Contrary, And I Thank God heer Mo. I hope
may be well Assured of their goodnes. yet euery thyng hath his Tyme and
must be helped as ned requyreth

My L I haue one meange to Carry Away all the offysers that owe to me
but Sir W. Wynter I take Mr. Hawkyns and Mr. Edward lathynde to
wayt on yow L and to put the 4 gaud shyppes in Redynes. Any thyng
shall gradly ned yf the Spanysh forses Come out, and so cry to
troyllyng no mor tym to troygthe at large lyvyng under suche I dar
yow L most hublle farewell the 22 of Fe at 12 A clok the After noon

6   THE ARK ROYAL

The last paragraph of another letter from the Lord Admiral to Burghley praising the condition of the Queen's ships, and his own flagship in particular.

... I proteste before god and as my soule shall answere for it that I thinke there were neaver in any place in the world worthier shippes than theise are for soe manye. And as fewe as we are if the Kinge of Spaines forces be not hunderethes we will make good sporte w[i]th them. And I praie your Lo[rdship] tell her ma[jes]tie from me that her moneye was well geaven for the Arke Rawlye[1], for I thinke her the odd ship in the worlde for all conditiones, and trewly I thinke there can noe greate ship make me change and goe oute of her. We can see noe saile greate nor small but howe far soeaver theye be of, we fetche them and speake w[i]th them. And soe I bid youre L[ordshi]p moste hartely farewell. from aboard her ma[jes]t[y's] good ship the Arke the laste of februarie 1587[2]

youre L[ordshi]ps most assured to comand
C. Howard

State Papers Domestic, 1588, SP 12/208 No.87, f. 201v
1   The ship had been bought by the Queen from Sir Walter Raleigh.
2   1588 New Style.

I professe before god And as my sowle shall answere for it that I
thinke there were never navey in any place in the world worthier
shipped then theise are for so many. And as sone as doe have
is thinkinge of Spaines force be not syndewethe we will make
good sporte with them And I praye you tell her ma. from me
that her money was well geaven for the Arke Rawlye, for
I thinke her the odd ship in the worlde for all conditiones, And
trowly I thinke there can no greate ship make me chaunge
And goe oute of her. we can see no saile greate nor small
but howe far socauer theye be off, we fetche them and speake
with them. and so I bid youre lp. moste hartely farewell. from aboard
her mat good ship the Arke the laste of februarie 1587

youre lp most assured
To Comand

Howard

41

7   DRAKE'S STRATEGY

Drake writes to the Privy Council urging that the Armada be attacked before it sails.

Right honorable, and my verie good Lordes; understandinge by yo[u]r good LL[ordship]s L[ett]res, her Ma[jes]t[y]s goode inclynac[i]on for the speedye sendinge of theise forces here, unto the seas, for the defence of thenemy, and that of her Ma[jes]t[y]s greate favor, and yo[u]r LL[ordship]s good opynyon, you have made choice of me (althoughe the leaste of many) to be as an Actor in so greate a cause; I am moste humblie to beseeche my moste gracious Soveraigne and yo[u]r good LL[ordship]s to heare my poore opynyon, w[i]th favor, and to Judge of it accordinge to yo[u]r greate wisdomes.

If her Ma[jes]tie, and yo[u]r LL[ordship]s thinke, that the K[ing] of Spaigne meanethe any invasyon in Englande, then doubtlesse, his force is, and wilbe greate in Spaigne, and thereon he will make his groundworke, or foundation, whereby the prynce of Parma maye have the better entraunce, w[hi]ch in myne owne Judgemente, is moste to be feared; But if there maye be suche a staye or stoppe made, by any meanes, of this ffleete in Spaigne, that they maye not come throughe the seas, as conquerors (w[hi]ch I assure my selfe, they thincke to doe) then shall the prince of Parma, have suche a checke therebye, as were meett.

To prevente this, I thinke it goode, that theise forces here, should be made as stronge, as to yo[u]r H[onours'] wisdomes shalbe thoughte convenyente, and that for two speciall causes: ffirste, for that they are like, to strike the firste blowe, and secondlie, it will putt greate and goode hartes, into her Ma[jes]t[y]s lovinge subiects, bothe abroade and at home; ffor that they wilbe p[er]swaded in conscyence, that the Lorde of all strengthes, will putt into her Ma[jes]tie, and her people, coraige, and boldnes, not to feare any invasyon in her owne Countrie, but to seeke Gods enemyes and her Ma[jes]t[y]s, where they maye be founde: ffor the Lorde is one our side, whereby we maye assure o[u]r selves, o[u]r nombres are greater than theirs. I muste crave p[ar]done of yo[u]r good Ll[ordship]s, againe and againe, for, my conscience hath caused me, to putt my pen to the pap[er], and as, God in his goodnes, hathe putt my hande to the ploughe, so in his mercy he will never suffer me, to turne backe from the truthe.

My verie good LL[ordship]s, nexte under Gods mightie protect[i]on, the advantaige and gaine of tyme and place, wilbe the onlie & cheife meane, for o[u]r goode, wherein I most humblie beseech yo[u]r good LL[ordship]s to p[er]sever, as you have began, for that w[i]th feiftie saile of shippinge, we shall doe more good uppon their owne Coaste, then a greate manye more, will doe here at home, and the sooner we are gone, the better we shalbe able to ympeache them.

There is come home. synce the sendinge awaie of my laste messenger, one bark (whome I sente out as an Espiall[1],) who confyrmeth those intelligencs, whereof I have advertized yo[u]r LL[ordship]s by him: and that divers of those Biskaines[2] are abroade uppon that coaste, wearinge Englishe flagges, whereof there are made in Lisbone three hundreth, w[i]th the redde Crosse, w[hi]ch is so greate presumpc[i]on, preceedinge of the hautynes & pride of the Spayniarde, and not to be tollerated, by any true naturall Englishe harte:

I have herein enclosed, sente this note unto yo[u]r LL[ordship]s to consider if our proporc[]ione, in powlder, shotte and other munyc[i]on, under the hande of the Surveyors Clerke of the ordynaunce; the w[hi]ch proporc[i]on in powlder and shotte, for o[u]r greate ordynaunce in her Ma[jes]t[y]s shippes, is but for one daie and halfes servyce, if it be begonne & contynewed, as the service maye requyer; and but five lastes of powlder[3] for xxiiii saile of the marchaunte shipes, w[hi]ch will scante be suffytyent for one daies service, as divers occasyons maye be offred: Good my LL[ord]s I beseeche yo[u], to consider deeplie of this, for it importeth but the losse of all.

State Papers Domestic, 1588, SP 12/209 No.40, f. 77

1   A scout or spy.
2   Biscayners; Basques, ships of Biscay or Vizcaya province.
3   The last of powder was 24 barrels of 100 lbs. each.

I have staied this messenger somewhat the longer[4], for the hearinge of this Dutcheman, who came latelie out of Lisbone; and hath delivered theise advertisements, herein enclosed, under his hande the 28th of this Marche, before my selfe and divers Justics:

I have sente unto yo[u]r good LL[ordship]s the note of suche powlder and munytyon, as are delivered unto us for this great service, w[hi]ch in truthe I Judge to be iuste a thirde p[ar]te, of that w[hi]ch is needefull; ffor if we should wante it, when we shall have moste neede thereof, it wilbe too late to sende to the Tower[5] for it; I assure yo[u]r Ho[nours] it neither is or shalbe spente in vaine. And thus restinge at yo[u]r Ho[nours] it neither is or shalbe spente in vaine. And thus restinge at yo[u]r H[onours'] father direc[i]on, I humblie take my leave of yo[u]r good LL[ordship]s, ffrom Plymowth this xxxth of marche 1588:

Yo[u]r good LL[ordship]s verie readie
to be comaunded:
Fra: Drake

4   The last two paragraphs are added by the same hand but in a different ink.

5   The Tower of London housed the principal powder magazine.

40

Right honorable, and my verie good Lordes: vnderstandinge by yo[ur] good LL[ordshippes] L[ett]res,
h[er] Ma[ies]t[ie] good inclynation for the speedye sendinge of these forces here,
vnto the seas, for the defence of the countrye, and that of h[er] Ma[ies]t[ie] gratius
favor, and yo[ur] LL[ordshippes] good opynyon, you have made mynd of me (althoughe
the leaste of many) to be as an instrument in so greate a cause: I am
moste humblie to beseeche my moste gratius Soberaigne and yo[ur] good
LL[ordshippes] to heare my poore opynyon notwithstandinge, and so to iudge of it accordinge
to yo[ur] greate wisdomes.

58

If her Ma[ies]t[ie] and yo[ur] LL[ordshippes] thinke that the k[inge] of Spaigne
meaneth any invasyon in England, then doubtles he, this forces is and
wilbe greate in Spaigne, and therein he will make his ground worke
or foundation, whereby the pryme of Parma maye have the
better entrance with in myne owne iudgement, is moste to be
feared; But if there maye be suche a staye or stoppe made, by
any meanes of this fleete in Spaigne, that they maye not come
throughe the seas, at conquerors (w[hi]ch I assure my selfe, they thinke
to doe) then shall the prynce of Parma, have suche a checke
therebye, as were meete:

To prevente this, I thinke it goode, that these forces here,
should be made as stronge, as to yo[ur] LL[ordshippes] wisdomes shalbe thoughte
convenyent, and that for two speciall causes: firste, for that they
are like, to strike the firste blowe, and stronglie, it will putt greate
and good hartes, into her Ma[ies]t[ie] lovinge subiectes, bothe abroade and
at home; for that they wilbe perswaded in conscience, that the
Lorde of all strengthe, will putt into her Ma[ies]t[ie] and her people, e
corage and bolenes, not to feare any invasyon in her owne
countrie but to seeke Gods enemyes and her Ma[ies]t[ie] wh[er]e they
maye be founde: for the Lorde is one our side, wherebye we
maye assure o[ur] selves, o[ur] nombers are greater then theirs: I muste
crave pardon of yo[ur] good LL[ordshippes] againe and againe, for, my conscience
hath caused me to putt my pen to the paper, and as God in
his goodnes, hath putt my hande to the plough, so in his mercy
he will never suffer me, to turne backe from the truthe:

My verie good LL[ordshippes], next vnder Gods mightie protection, the
advantaige and gaine of tyme and place, wilbe the onlye o[ur] refuge,
meanes for o[ur] goode, wherein I most humblie beseeche yo[ur] good LL[ordshippes] to
vse o[ur] tyme, as yo[ur] have begun, for that with thirtie saile of shippinge
we shall doe more good vppon their owne coaste, then a greate
manye more, will doe here at home, and the sooner we are gone,
the better we shalbe able to ymploye them.

There is come home, synce the sendinge awaie of my laste
mes[sen]ger (whom I doubte not as an es[pia]ll) who confirmeth
those intelligences, whereof I have advertized yo[ur] LL[ordshippes] by him:
and that divers of those Brittaines are abroade vppon that
coaste, wearinge Englishe flagges, whereof there are made in
Lisbone three hunderte, w[i]th the redde crosse, w[hi]ch is a
greate presumption, proceedinge of the haultines & pride of the
Spanyardes, and not to be tollerated, by any true naturall
Englishe harte:

I have herein enclosed, sente this note vnto yor LLps to consider of our e
proportions, in powder, Shotte and other municyon, vnder the hande of
the Surveyor of the ordynaunce; the wch proportion in powder
and Shotte for or greate ordynaunce in his Maties Shippes, is but for
one daie and halfe servise, yf it be by some 3ly contynued, as
the servise maye require; and lesse store of powder for
ev'y Saile of the marchaunte Shippes, wch will scante be
sufficyent for one daies servise as dyvers occasyons maye be
offered. good my Lps I beseche yow, to consider deeplie of this,
for it importithe but the loss of all.

I have staied this messenger somewhat the longer, for the beakinge
of this spanyarde who came latelie out of lisbone, and hath deliuered
these advertisemtes, herein enclosed, vnder his hande the 28th of this
Marche, before my selfe and dyvers Justice.

I have sente vnto yor good LLps the note of suge powder, and
municyon, as are deliuered vnto vs for this greate servise wch in
truthe I Judge to be Juste a thirde parte, of that wch is nedefull,
for if we should wante it when we shall have moste nede
thereof, it wilbe too late to sende to the Tower for it; I assure
yor Lo: it neither is or shalbe spente in vaine. And
thus restinge at yor Lo: harde direction, I humblie take my
leave of yor good LLps from My house this xxxth of Marche
1588.

yor good LLps service readie
to be comaunded:

8 NAVAL INTELLIGENCE

It was impossible to conceal the preparation of the Armada, and the English received frequent 'advertisements' of Spanish progress, not all of them as accurate as this intercepted letter:

By l[ett]res written from Lisbon the 7 of May stilo nuovo[1] by a Captain of an Italian shippe serving in the Spanish fleet, it is advertised th[at] at that instant all thinges were in readines for the departure of the fleet th[at] all both soldiors and shippes had receaved two monthes pay, having due above seven.

In the said Captaines shippe were imbarked Don Alonso di Lieva[2] generall of the Spanish footmen and with him to the number of 700 soldiors and mariners w[hi]ch are about *150*. That they had taken in five peeces of Artigliery above the ordinary furniture of the shippe w[hi]ch were great. That the whole fleet consisteth of between 125 and 130 vesselles great and small. The great shippes are about 73. There are also 4 galeasses and 4 gallyes[3]. The number of the soldiors between ten and eleven thowsand besides the marriners. although it be given out that they are a great manie more.

The Duke of Medina Sidonia is generall of the entireprise, accompanied with a good number of gent[lemen].

A curri[e]r come from Spaigne and passed thorough Roan[4] to the Duke of Parma, reported for certain th[at] the fleet were departed from Lisbona.

In Calais there is arrived a Spanish Shippe w[hi]ch departed from Lisbona fower dayes after the fleet w[hi]ch may be an argument th[at] not want of winde but for some other cause it stayeth at the Groyne.[5]

State Papers Spain, 1588, SP 94/3, f. 227r
1 New style; according to the Gregorian Calendar adopted by the Catholic states, which was ten days ahead of the Julian Calendar still used in England, and began the year on 1st January instead of Lady Day (25th March).
2 Don Alonso de Leiva sailed in the carrack *La Rata Coronada*
3 The four galleys sailed with the Armada, but turned back after meeting heavy weather in the Bay of Biscay.
4 Rouen.
5 After leaving Lisbon the Armada was damaged and scattered by a gale, and reassembled at Corunna.

By lres written from Lisbon the 7 of May stilo novo by a Captaine of an Italian shippe serving in the Spanish fleet, it is advertised that at that instant all thinges were in readines for the departure of the fleet. That all the soldiers and shippes had rec and two monethes pay: having due above seven.

In the said Captaines shippe were imbarked Don Alonso di Leiua generall of the Spanish footmen and with him to the nomber of 700 soldiers and mariners which are about 150. That they had taken in store yardes of Artillery above the ordinary furniture of the shippe very was great. That the whole fleet consisteth of betwene 125 and 130 vessells great and smale. The great shippes are about 73. There are also 4 galeasses and 4 gallyes. The nomber of the soldiers betwene ten and eleven thousand besides the mariners. Although it be given out that there are a great number more.

The Duke of Medina Sidonia is generall of the entire enterprise, and is armed with a good number of servants.

A courrier went from ... and passed through from to the Duke of Parma, and reported for certaine that the fleet were departed from Lisbon.

In Calais there is arrived a Spanish shippe which departed from Lisbon fower dayes after the fleet which may be an argument that not for want of winde but for some other cause, is stayeth in the Groyne.

227

By the middle of July when Burghley wrote this letter to Walsingham the English government was in desperate straits for money to keep the fleet at sea.

S[i]r I fynd my my[n]d, as much troubled to wryte as now I do as co[mm]only my stomak is ageynst purgy[n]g; but I ca[n] not co[n]cele fro[m] you the causes, W[hi]c[h] will shortly bry[n]g forth desp[er]at effects.

I have receaved let[er]s fro[m] my L[ord] admyrall and Mr Hawky[n]s, w[it]h a cedule declary[n]g that they have great lack of mo[n]y for wag[e]s, beside victells for w[hi]c[h] Quarles hath vj^m[1] this last week.

and now Mr Hawky[n]s declaratio[n], that to mak a full pay to the 28 of this mo[n]th ther must be payd xix^m lxx li[2] and of the vj^m li[3] which he had ther remayneth w[it]h hy[m] but v^c li[4]. I marvell th[a]t wher so many ar dead o[n] the seas the paye is not dead w[it]h the[m] or w[it]h many of the[m][5]

And how the reckoning for victells will fall out I know not. but I feare the vi^m li[6] will not s[er]ve. and yet as I p[er]ceave my L[ord] Admyralls Co[m]pany ar victelled untill midd August. and if S[ir] fr[ancis] drake war victelled his L[ordship] might go to the sea w[it]out delaye.

At this tyme also is dema[n]ded by the office of the Admyralte, for to pay an old dett for p[ro]visio[n]s vij^m li and to restor ther lacks vj^m in toto xiij^m.[7] and I have moved the[m] to content the creditors, for the vij^m w[ith] on thryd now. on oth[er] third in the end of Aug[ust]. and the later at Michelmas[8] w[hi]c[h] is a charitable releff. and so ther might [be] lesur in payi[n]g the other vj^m li for new p[ro]visio[n]s.

Ther is also payd to Quarles for j mo[n]ths victell for the shipps in the narrow seas j^m viij^c liiij li.[9]

The office of the ordona[n]ce dema[n]deth for furniture of habillements &c for to s[er]ve an army by la[n]d about viij^m.[10] ther is also besyde ij^m vij^c li[11] lately payd to the Creditors, the so[m]e of ij^m iiij^c lxxix li[12] to be payd.

I know the ij towns and the army have also great nede of mo[n]ey.

A ma[n] wold wish if peace ca[n] not be had, that the enemy wold not longar delay, but prove, (as I trust) his evill fortune. for as these expectatio[n]s do consume us. so I wold hope by Gods goodness uppo[n] ther defect, we might have on half yers tyme to provyde for mony.[13]

I have had Confere[n]ce w[it]h pallavicino and w[it]h saltenstall[14] how 40 or 50^m might be had for x p[er] Cento. but I fynd no p[ro]babillite, how to gett mony here in specie w[hi]c[h] is our lack. but by escha[n]dg to have it out of the p[ar]ts beyo[n]d sea w[hi]c[h] will not be done but in a lo[n]g tyme.

yet ther is so[m]e lykhood th[a]t our M[er]cha[n]ts of stade,[15] might practise for xx or xxx^m[16] for which ther shall be so[m]e proff[it] very secretly.

I shall but fill my l[ett]re w[it]h more Mela[n]choly matter, if I shuld reme[m]ber what mony must be had to paye v^m footme[n] and j^m horsme[n] for defe[n]ce of the enemy la[n]dy[n]g in Essex.

Yours most assur[ed]
W. Burghley

State Papers Domestic, 19th July 1588: SP 12/212 No.66, f. 139, holograph
1 £6,000.
2 £19,070.
3 £6,000.
4 £500.
5 Added in the margin.
6 £6,000
7 £7,000 and £6,000, in all £13,000.
8 29th September.
9 £1,854.
10 £8,000.
11 £2,700.
12 £2,479.
13 i.e. if the Spaniards would only try their fortunes at once and be defeated, the English might have six months' breathing space to find money.
14 Sir Horatio Palavicino and Richard Saltonstall, prominent London merchants.
15 The English merchant colony at Stade, on the Elbe near Hamburg.
16 £20,000 or £30,000.

Sr I fynd my mynd, as much trobled to wryte as now I doo
as earstly my stomak is agaynst purgyng. but I can
not edeale to yow the cares, wch will hortly bryng
forth despat effecte.

I have receaved las fro my L. Admyrall and Mr
Hawkys, wt a letter declaryng that they have great
lack of mony for way, besyde vidtells for wch Quarles
hath vigᵃ this last weke

and now Mr Hawkys declaratio, that to make a
full pay to yᵉ 28ᵗʰ of this moth ther must be
payd xix ᵗhxet end of yᵉ vigᵃ which he had ther
remayneth in hs but viₗ

I marvell yᵗ wher so many
ar ded to yᵉ bers
the paye is lost
ded wt the oo it
many of the

And how yᵉ reckonyng for vidtells wll fall out
I knowe not. but I leave yᵉ vigᵃ wll not yet.
and yet as I perave my L. Admyralls Cpany sav vidtelld
untill midd Agust. and if yᵗ L so dodk way vidtelld
his L might go to yᵉ sea wthot delave

At this tyme also is demaded by yᵉ offier of yᵉ Admyralte, to
pay an old dett for pensos Lvigᵃ end to vesher thau
debts vigᵃ in toto xvigᵃ and I have moved the to
contrull yᵉ credetors, for yᵉ Lvigᵃ wᵗ on thyrd woar cu olt
thred in yᵉ end of Avg. and yᵉ later for Michelmas
wᵗ is a charitable releff. and so ther might lyve in pay xⁱy

yͤ other vij. for new pvices

Ther is also payd to Quarles for yͤ mothe victill for yͤ
shipps in yͤ narrow seas — ij vij ͬ lxvij ͬ

The office of yͤ ordonace demadeth for furniture of habilim͠tͭ
ordr for to hae an army by lad: about vij ᵐ

ther is also beside yͭ vij lately payd to yͤ creditors, yͭ dͭ of
army shoeur will be payd

I know yͭ ij townes and yͤ army have also great nede of mony.

I ma wold wish it preier en not be had, that other the
enemy wold knot lenger delay, but prove, as I trust his
evill fortune. for as these expeḍtations do consue vs.
so I wold hope by gods gooḍnes vppo ther deeḍ, we mȳght
have on half yeas tyme to provyde for mony.

I have had conferēc wt pallaviciav. and wt Salleastell: how
40. or 50 ᵐl mȳght be had for x.p ͭ cento. but I gͤ
no ghavilite, how to gett mony here in preie wt is our
lack. but by seauery to shave it ovt bef yͤ ph beyͦd sea
wͭ will not be done in a loy tyme
yet ther is for lykehod if our ᵐsChaḷ of Stade, mȳght
practis for xx or xxxͤ for whoth ther shal be for
profit very sevyly.

I hall but till my lre is move melaencly maher, if I hall vene bvt
what eha mony must be had to puvv vay fathim and yͤ hͦyfaḷ
for defer of yͤ emny ladgṉ wt ij ᵐx

10 THE ARMADA IS SIGHTED

Howard's brief report to Walsingham of the first action.

S[i]r I will not trouble you w[i]th anie longe l[ett]re we are at this p[re]sent otherwise occupied then w[i]th writinge. Uppo[n] ffridaie at Plymouthe I receaved intelligence that there were a greate number of ships descried of[f] of the Lisarde wheruppo[n] althoughe the winde was verie skante we firste warped oute of harbro that nyghte and uppo[n] Saterdaie turned oute verie hardly[1] the winde beinge at Southe Weste and aboute 3 of the clo[ck] in the afternone descried the Spanishe fleete and [   ][2] did what we could to worke for the wind w[hi]ch [   ] morninge we had recovered. discryinge theire f[leet ?] consiste of 120 saile whereof there are 4 g[alleasses ?] and many ships of greate burthen. At nine of th[e] [clock ?] we gave them feighte w[hi]ch contynewed untill on[e ?   ] feighte we made som of them to beare Roome to stop the[ir ?] leaks not w[i]thstandinge we durste not adventure to put in amongste them theire fleete beinge soe stronge But there shall nothinge be eather neglected or unhasarded that may worke theire overthrowe.

S[i]r the captaines in her ma[jes]t[y]s ships have behaved them selves moste bravely and like me[n] hitherto and I doubte not will contynewe to theire greate comendac[i]on. And soe recome[n]din[g] oure good successe to yo[u]r godlie praiers I bid you hartelie farewell. from aboard the Arke thwarte of Plymmouthe the 21 of Julie 1588

youre verie lovinge freind

C. Howard

Sir The Southerly wynde That brought us bak fro[m] The cost of spayne brought The[m] out God blessed us w[ith] Torny[n]g us bak. Sir for The love of God and our Country let us have w[ith] some sped some graet Shot sent us of all begnes[3]. for This sarvis wyll Contynue long and some powder w[ith] it

State Papers Domestic, SP 12/212 No.80, f. 167, holograph postcript

1   i.e. beat out with difficulty.
2   A piece of the manuscript is torn off.
3   i.e. of each size.

Sr I will not trouble you wth anie longe lre we are at this psent
otherwise occupied then wth writinge vppon fridaie last the
monthe I receaved intelligence that there were a greate number
of shipps descried off of the lisarde wherevppon althoughe the
winde was verie skante we first warpped oute wth our shipps
that nyghte and vppon saterdaie turned oute verie hardly
the winde beinge at sowthwest and aboute 3 of the clock
in the afternone descried the Spanishe fleete and
did what we coulde to worke for the winde wch
morninge we thus recovered. discryinge there
to consiste of 120. saile wherof there are 4 g-
and many shipps of greate burthen. At nine of the
we gave them fighte wch continewed vntile one
fighte we made som of them to beare rome to stop the
leake notwthstandinge we durste not adventure to put in
amongste them there fleete beinge soe stronge But there
shall nothinge be eather neglected or vnhazarded that may
worke there overthrowe.

Sr the captaines in her maty shipps have behaved themselves
moste bravely and like men hetherto and I doubte not will
continewe to there greate comendacion. And soe recomendin
our good successe to god lie praiers I bid you hartie
lie farewell. from aboard the arke the arke wher of
god lie in moneth the 21 of Julie 1588

your verie lovinge freind
[signature: Ho Howard]

Sir the sowtherly wynde that
broughte vs backe fro the cost of
spayne broughte them oure God blesse
vs wt tomorowe vs back. Sir for the
lorde of God and our Country lett vs have
wt some spud some greate shot sent vs
of all beynes. for this service wyll coste
powder wt

11　ACTION OFF THE ISLE OF WIGHT

Sir George Carey, Governor of the island, reports the fighting to the Earl of Sussex, Lord Lieutenant of Hampshire. Carey was a landman viewing the battle from a distance, but his impression of very heavy but rather ineffectual cannonading seems to have been correct.

　　may it please yo[u]r L[ordship] to understand that finding by yours the copy and direction of the LL[ords'] l[ett]res[1] for supplying the L[ord] Admiralls wantes touching that I have thus farre proceeded two daies since I sent his Lo[rdship] 4 shippes and a pinnace sufficiently furnished w[i]th mariners and soldiours from whome I have not yet hard any newes but sending yesterday an other pinnace unto him w[i]th an hundred men he returned them unto me this afternoone w[i]th great thankes willing the Captaine to tell me that he had as many men as he desired or could well use. for yo[u]r L[ordshi]ps newes I humbly thanke you.

　　This morning began a great fight betwixt both fleetes south of this Iland 6 leagues[2] w[hi]ch continued from five of the clocke untill tenne w[i]th so great expence of powder and bullet that during the said time the shott continued so thicke together that it might rather have beene iudged a skirmish w[i]th small shott on land then a fight w[i]th great shott on sea in w[hi]ch conflict thankes be to god there hath not bene two of our men hurt.

　　The newes in the fleett are my L[ord] Harry Seymor is hardly laide unto by the Dunkerkers and that Scilla is taken by the french or the spanish.[3]

　　The fleetes keepe the direct trade[4] and shott into the sea out of o[u]r sight by three of the clocke this afternoone whereupon we have dissolved o[u]r campe wherein we have continued since Monday. And so prayeing yo[u]r LL[ordshi]p to send this enclosed by the post[5] I humbly commit you to God from Carisbrooke castle this 25 of July at 8 howres in the night

Your ll[ordshi]ps to Com[m]aunde
George Carey

State Papers Domestic;
SP 12/213 No.40,i, f. 97
1　i.e. finding by your copies of the Privy Council's letters their directions...
2　18 miles, but the distance cannot have been anything like so great.
3　Neither rumour was true; Seymour had not been attacked by the Spanish from Dunkirk, nor had the Isles of Scilly been taken.
4　i.e. kept in the main fairway up the Channel.
5　To the Privy Council.

Vera Copia:

May it please yo L: to understand that finding by yours the copy, and direction of the LL: these for supplying the L: Admiralls wantes touching that I have sins favour proceeded two dais since I sent his Lo: 4 shippes and a pinnace sufficiently furnished with mariners and soldiours from whome I have not yet hard any newes but sending my yesterday an other pinnace unto him with two hundred men he returned them unto me this afternoone with great thankes willing the Captaine to tell me that he had as many men as he desired or could well use. for yo Lyt newes I humbly thanke you.

This morning began a great fight betwixt both fleetes south of this Iland 6 leagues which continued from five of the clocke untill time with so great expence of powder and ballet that during the said time the shott continued so thicke togeather that it might rather have bene judged a skirmish with small shott on land then a fight with great shott on sea in which conflict thanked be to god there hath not bene two of our men hurt.

The newes in the fleett are my L: Harry Seymor is hardly laide bado by the Dunkerkers and that Scilla is taken by the freuch or the spanish

The fleetes keepe their direct trade and shott into the sea out of o sight by three of the clocke this afternoone whereupon we have dissolved o campe wherein we have continued since monday, And so praying yo Ll to send this enclosed by the post I humbly comitt you to god from Carisbrooke castle this 25 of July at 8 howers in the night

Your Llps to Comaunde
George Carey

Howard reports to Walsingham on the evening of the battle; the critical shortage of food and ammunition was uppermost in his mind, and it was as yet far from clear that he had won a great victory and turned the course of the campaign.

Sir I have receaved yo[u]r l[ett]re wherin you desire a p[ro]portione of shot and poder[1] to be set downe by me and sente unto you w[hi]ch by reason of the uncertaintie of the service noe ma[n] can doe therfore I praie you to send w[i]thall speed as muche as you ca[n]. And bicause som of o[u]r ships are victualed but for a verie shorte time and my Lo[rd] Henry Seymor w[i]th his companie not for one daie in like to praie you[2] to dispache awaie o[u]r victuales w[i]th all possible speed bicause we knowe not whether[3] we shalbe driven to pursue the Spa[nish] fleete.

This morninge we drave a gallias ashore before Callis whether I sent my longeboate to board her where divers of my me[n] were slaine and my leiftenante sore hurte in the takinge of her Eaver since we have chased them in feighte untill this eaveninge late and distressed them mutche: but there fleete consistethe of mightie ships and greate strengthe yet we doubte not by godes good asistance to oppresse them and so I bid you hartely farewell from aboarde her ma[jes]t[y]s good ship the Arke the 29 of Julye 1588

yo[u]r very lovinge freind

C. Howard

Sir I wyll not wryghte unto heer mage[s]t[y] befor mor be downe Ther forse is wonderfull gret and strong And yet we ploke Ther fethers by lyttell and littell I pray to god That The forses of The land be strong A nuf To Annser so pusant[4] A forse. Ther is not on Flushynger nor Holender at The Sies.[5]

S[i]r I have taken the cheefe Galias this daie before Callis w[i]th the losse of divers of my men. But Mo[nsieur] Gorden[6] dothe detaine her as I heare saye I cold not send unto hym bicause I was in feighte therfore I praie you to write unto him eather to deliver her or at least wise to p[ro]mise uppo[n] his honoure that hie will not yeald her up againe unto the enemye

State Papers Domestic; SP 12/213 No.64, f. 148; 1st postscript holograph, 2nd on a separate scrap of paper

1   i.e. an estimate of requirements.
2   i.e. I am in like manner to pray you...
3   Whither, as below.
4   Puissant.
5   This was unfair; the Dutch were patrolling their coastal waters, out of sight of the English.
6   Gourdan, the governor of Calais.

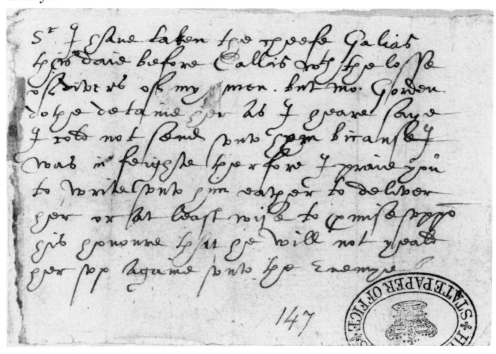

1st postscript ▷

◁ 2nd postscript

Sir I have received yor the messenger you desire to por=
tione of shot and powder to be set downe by me
and sente unto you. wch by reason of the pre=
sante of the service no ma rande therfore
I praye you to sende wth all speed as muche
as you ca. And trans som of yor shipps be
sp written but for a verie shorte time and my
Lo. Henry Seymor wth shipps come not for ome
dayes in like to praye you to disparse anone
or sp written wth all possible speed bicause
we knowe not wch se we shalbe driven
to pursue the Sp. fleete.

This morninge we drave a gallias ashore before
Callis whereof I sent my longeboate to boord the
whereof divers of my me were slaine and my
lieutenante sore hurte in the takinge of her.
Ebbor since we have chased them in foruffe
untill this eveninge late and distressed them
muche: but there fleete consiste of mightie
ships and greate strenghe yet we doubte not
by godds good assistance to oppresse them and so I
bid you hartely farewell. from abord her ma:
good Ship the Arke the 29. of July. 1588

yor poore lovinge freind

Howard

Sir I will not wryghte unto heer
magesty befor nor be dewens
Ther force is wonderfull gret
and strong And yet we plutter
Ther fethers by lyttell and lyttell
I pray to god that the forses on
the land be strong A ryse to Armey
So ynsure A ysorb. Ther is not on flushynger nor Holander
at the sees

148

13 DRAKE ON THE BATTLE OF GRAVELINES

Drake's note to Walsingham is briefer and more cheerful than the Lord Admiral's, but he too clearly had no idea that the real fighting was over.

Right ho[nourable] this bearer cam a board the ship I was in in a wonderffull good tyme and brought w[it]h hym as good knowlege, as we culd wyshe, his carffullnes therein is worthy recompence, for that god hath geven us so good a daye in forecynge the enemy so far to Leeward. as I hope in god the prince of parma: and the duke of Medonya, shall not shake hands this ffewe dayes, and when so ever they shall meet. I beleve nether of them will greatly reioyce of this dayes Servis, the towne of callys, hath seene sum p[ar]te thereof, whose mayor her ma[jes]tie is beholding unto: busines comandes me to end, god blesse her ma[jes]tie our gracious Sovraygne and geve us all grace to leve in his feare. I assure yo[u]r ho[nour] this dayes Servis hath mych apald the enemy, & no doubt but incoraiged our armey, from a board her ma[jes]ties good ship the revenge the 29th July 1588

yo[u]r ho[nour's] most redy to be com[m]anded
Fra: Drake

ther must be great care taken to send us monytyon and vittuall whether so ever the enemy goeth.

yo[u]rs
Fra: Drake

State Papers Domestic; SP 12/213 No.65, f. 150, holograph

Right ho: this bearer cam a bord the ship that
... in a wondeffull good tyme. and brought
... us ... ab god knowe[g], ab no ...
... the ... ... it wor[th]
... for that god ...
... good a day ...
... ... heward, ab I ...
... the prince of parma. and the
duke of ... shall not ...
... the fleet ... and
... to obey ... shall meet ...
... will ...
... of ... ... the
town of ...
... ...
... late[s]: ...
... god bleff ...
... and ... to all ...
... the ... fleet ...
... ... no doubt ...
... our ... from a bord
... ... 1533 ... ... most
... to be command[ed]
Fra: Vvale

Two days after Gravelines, Hawkins sent Walsingham his account of the campaign so far. Like all the English commanders, he believed the crisis of the fighting was still to come.

my bounden duty humbly reme|m|bred unto yo|u|r good Lo|rd|sh|ip|. I have not busyed my sealf to write often to yo|u|r Lo|rd|sh|ip| in this great cause, for that my Lo|rd| Admyrall, dothe continuallye advertise the manor of all things that dothe passe. So doe others that understande the state of all things aswell as my sealf.

we mett w|i|th this fleet, somewhat to the westwarde of Plymoth upon sondaye in the morning, being the 21 of Julye wheare we had some smale fight withe the|m| in the after none. By the cominge aboarde one of the other of the spaniards, a great shipe a Biscane|r|, spent hir formast, & boxsprite, which was left by the fleet in the sea, and so taken up by S|i|r ffrauncis Drake the next morninge.

The same sondaye ther was by a fyer Chauncing by a barell of powder a great Biscane spoyled and abandoned, w|hi|ch my Lo|rd| tooke up and sent awaye.

The tuesdaye following athwarte of portland, we had a sharpe and long fight w|i|th them, wherein we spent a great parte of our powder and shott, so as it was not thought good to deale w|i|th the|m| any more, till that was releved.

The thrusdaye followinge by the occasion of the schateringe of one of the great ships fro|m| the fleet, w|hi|ch we hoped to have cutt of, ther grew a hot fraye, wherein some store of powder was spent, and after that litell done till we came neere to Callis, wheare the fleet of spaine Ankered and our fleet by them, and because they should not be in peace, ther to refresh ther water, or to have conference w|i|th those of the Duke of Parmas partie, my Lo|rd| Admyrall w|i|th fyring of ships, determined to remove them, as he did, and put the|m| to the seas, In w|hi|ch broile the Cheife galliasse spoyled hir rother, and so rowed ashore neere the towne of Callis, wheare she was possessed w|i|th of our men, but so agrounde, as she could not be brought awaye.

That morning being mondaye the 29 of Julie we folowed the spaniards & all that daye had w|i|th the|m| a longe and great figtht, wherein ther was great valure shewed generally of our company in this Battaile, ther was spent very much of o|u|r powder and shot, and so the winde begane to growe westarlye, a fresh gale and the spaniards put the|m| The|m|[1] sealves somwhat to the northwarde, wheare we follow and keepe co|m|pany w|i|th them, in this fight ther was some hurt done amonge the spaniards.

A great ship of the gallions of Portingall, his rother spoyled, and so the fleet leaft hir in the sea. I doubt not but all these things are writen more att large to yo|u|r Lo|rd|sh|ip| then I can doe but this is the substance and materiall matter th|a|t hathe past.

Our ships god be thanked have receaved littell hurt, and are of great force to acco|m|panye the|m|, and of such advantage, th|a|t w|i|th some continuance at the seas, and sufficientlye p|ro|vided of shote and powder, we shalbe able w|i|th gods favour to wery the|m| oute of the sea and confound the|m|.

Yet as I gather Certainlye ther are amongest them 50 forcible and invincible ships, w|hi|ch consist of those that follow, viz 9 gallions of Portingall of 800 ton a peece saving 2 of the|m| are but 400 ton a peece 20 great venetians and Argosies[2] of the seas, w|i|thin the straight of 800 a peece.

One shipe of the Duke of fflorence of 800 ton.

20 great Biskane|r|s of 500 or 600 ton.

4 galliasses whearof one is in ffraunce.

Ther are 30 hulks[3] and 30 other smale ships, wherof littell accompte is to be made.

At ther departing from Lisborne being the 19 of maye by our accompt, they weare victualled for vj monethes, the|y| stayed in the groyne 28 dayes and ther refreshed ther

State Papers Domestic, SP 12/213 No.71, ff. 164-165. Postcript holograph
1   Word repeated at the turn-over of the page.
2   Argosies; ships of Ragusa, the merchant republic in Dalmatia.
3   Hulks; a type of merchant ship native to the Baltic.

water, at ther cominge from Lisborne, they weare taken w[i]th a flawe and 14 hulks or ther abouts cam neere ushante, and so retourned w[i]th Contrarye winds to the groyne and ther mett, and els ther was none other companye upon o[u]r cost, before the hole fleete arived. And in ther Cominge now a littell flaw tooke the[m] 50 leage from the Cost of Spaine, where one great ship was severed from them and iiij gallies, which hetherto, have not recovered ther Companye.

At ther dep[ar]ting fro[m] Lisborne the soldyers weare 20000 the mariners and others 8000 so as in all they weare 28000 men. Ther commissyon was to confer w[i]th the Prince of Parma (as I learne) and then to p[ro]ceed to the s[er]vice that should be ther concluded. And so the Duke to retourne into Spaine withe those ships and mariners and soldyars &c and ther furniture being lefte behinde.

nowe this fleet is heere and very forcible, and must be wayted upon withe all o[u]r force. which is littell ynoughe, ther would be an Infinite qua[n]tity of powder and shot p[ro]vided and contitinuallye [*sic*] sent aborde, w[i]thout the w[hi]ch great hasarde may growe to our Country, for this is the greatest and strongest co[m]binac[i]on to my understanding, that ever was gathered in Christendome, therefore I wishe it of all hands, to be mightelye and diligentlye loked into, and cared for.

The men have ben long unpayed and need releef, I pray yo[u]r Lo[rd]sh[ip] that the mony, that should have gone to Plymothe may now be sent to Dover, August now comethe in, and this cost will spend ground tackle, Cordage, Canvas and victualls, all w[hi]ch would be sent to dover in good plentye. withe these things and gods blessinge our kingdome maye be p[re]served w[hi]ch being neglected great hasard maye come. I write to yo[u]r Lo[rd]shipe bryeflye and playnlye, your wisdome and experience is great, But this is a matter far passing all that hathe been seene in our time or long before. And so praying to god for a hapye deliveraunce, fro[m] the malicious and dangerous practise of our enemys, I humblie take my leave from the sea aboarde the victorye. the Last of July 1588.

The spaniards take ther course for Schotland, my Lo[rd] dothe follow them. I doubt not w[i]th gods favour, but we shall impeache ther landinge, ther must be order for victuall, and mony powder and shot to be sent after us.

your Ll[ordship's] Humbly to comand
John Hawkyns

This is the coppy of the letter I send to my lord tresorer wher by I shall not nede to wryt to your honoure hellp us w[i]t[h] fournyturre & w[i]t[h] gods favour we shall confound ther devyces.

your Honours ever bownden
John Hawkyns

I pray your honour beare w[ith] this for yt ys done in hast & bad wetar. I.J.

my bounden duty humbly remembred vnto yo[ur] good Lo[rdshi]p. I haue
not busied my self to write often to yo[ur] Lo[rdshi]p in this great
cause, for that my Lo. Admyrall, dothe continuallye aduertise
the mane of all thinge that dothe passe. To doe others that
vnderstande the state of all thinge aswell as my self.

We mett w[i]th theis fleet, somewhat to the westwarde of Plymo[uth]
vpon sondaye in the morning, being the 21 of Julye whereon we
had some smale fight w[i]the the ni the after none. By the
cominge aboarde one of the other of the spaniarde, a great shipe
of Biscaie, spent hir formast, & boresprite, w[hi]ch was left
by the fleet in the sea, and so taken vp by S[i]r ffrauncis
Drake the next morninge.

The same sondaye there was by a fier chauncing by a
barrell of powder a great Biscaie spoyled and abandoned,
w[hi]ch my Lo. tooke vp and sent awaye.

The tuesdaye following a[s]twarte of portland, we had a
sharpe and long fight w[i]th them, wherein we spent a great
parte of our powder and shott, so as it was not thought good
to deale w[i]th the any more, till that was relieued.

The thursdaye following by the occasion of the scateringe
of one of the great shipe fro the fleet, w[hi]ch we hoped to
haue cutt of, then grew a hot fraye, wherein some store
of powder was spent, and after that litell done till we
came neere to Callis, where the fleet of spaine Ankered
and our fleet by them, and because they should not be in
peace, ther to refresh ther water, or to haue conference
w[i]th those of the duke of Parmas partie, my Lo. Admyrall
w[i]th firing of shipe, determined to remoue them, as he did
and put the to the seas, In w[hi]ch broile the cheife galliasse
spoyled hir rother, and so rowed ashore neere the towne
of Callis, where she was possessed of of our men, but
so agrounde, as she could not be brought awaye.

That morning being mondaye, the 29 of Julie we folowed
the spaniarde, all that daye had w[i]th the a longe and great
fight, wherein therwas great valure shewed generally
of our company in this Battaile, therwas spent very
much of o[ur] powder and shot, and so the winde began to
growe westerlye, a fresh gale and the spaniarde put the

(71)

somwhat
~north~

he sealneth to the ~northwarde~, wheare we follow and keepe companie
with them, in this fight ther was some hurt done amonge the
spaniardes.

A great shipp of the gallions of portingall, hir rother spoyled,
and so the fleet leaft hir in the sea, I doubt not but all these
thinge are written more att large to yor Loo. then I cann doo
but thisis the substance and materiall matter ytt hathe past.

Our shipp god be thanked have receaved littell hurt, and
are of great force to accompanye the, and of soch advantage, yt
with some contynuance at the sea, and sufficientlye prided of shote
and powder, we shalbe able wth good favour to wery the onte of
the sea and confound the.

Yet as I gather certainlye ther are amongest them so forcible
and invincible shipp, wch consist of these that follow, viz 9 gallions
of portingall of 800 ton a peece, to great venetians and argosies
of the seas, wthin the straightt of 800 a peece.

One shipp of the Duke of florence of 800 ton
10 great biscanes of 500 or 600 ton
4 galliasses wheareof one is in ffraunce.

Ther are 20 hulke and 20 other smale shipp, wheareof littell
attempte is to be made of.

At ther departing from Lisborne beinge the 19 of maye by on
attempt, they weare victualled for vj monethes, the stayed in
the groyne 28 dayes and ther refreshed ther water, at ther
cominge from Lisborne, they weare taken wth a flawe and 14
hulke or ther abonte came neere vshante, and so returned with
contrary winde to the groyne and ther mett, and els ther
was none other companye vpone a cost, before the hole fleete
arived. And in ther cominge now a littell flaw tooke the so
leave from the cost of Spaine, wheare one great ship was
severed from them and iiij galliots, which hetherto, have not
recovered ther companye.

At ther departing fro Lisborne the soldyers weare 20000 the
marinors and others 8000 so as in all they weare 28000 men.

Ther commission was to confer wth the prince of parma (as I
learne) and then to proceed to the state that shold be ther counties.
And so the Duke to returne into spaine with these ship
and marinors, the soldyars land and ther furniture beinge lefte
behinde.

nowe thisfleet is heere and very forcible, and must be wayted
vpon with all o^r force, wch is litell ynoughe, ther would
be an Infinite ~~company~~ quatity of powder and shot prided
and continuallye sent aborde, w^{th}out the wch great hasarde
may growe to o^r countery, for this is the greatest and strong
est combination to my vnderstanding, that euer was gathered
in christendome, therfore I wishe it off all handes, to be
mightelye and diligentlye Loked vnto, and cared for./

The men haue ben Long vnpayed and nedd releef, I pray
yor Lo^s that the mony that should haue gone to plymoth
may now be sent to Dover, I myst now remothe in, and
this cost will spend ground tackle, cordage, canvas and
~~these~~ vitnall, all wch would be sent to dober in good plentye./
with g^d and god blessing our kingdome maye be p^{ser}ued
wch beeing neglected great hasard maye come. I write to
yor Lo free bryshlye and playnlye, your wisdome and experienc
is great, But this is a matter far passing all that hath
been seene in our time or long before. And so prayyng
to god for a happye deliveraunce, fro the malicious and
dangerous practise of our enemyes, I humblie take my
Leave from the sea. aboarde the Victorye, the Last of Julii
1588./

The Spaniardes take ther course for scotland, ~~them~~ my Lo doth follow
them. I doubt not in gods fauour, but we shall impeache ther
Landinge, ther myst be order for vitnall, and mony powder
and shot sent after vs.

your L^l humbly to
comaund Iohn Hawkyns
~~I send to my Lord tresorer~~
~~who by~~ ~~I shall not nedi to~~ ~~w^{ryt} to your honour~~
~~thys wth wth my hand~~ ~~wth gods fauour we shall~~
~~comfound the devil./~~

your Honours euer bowad^s
I pray your honour bare w^{th}
this for y^t wth done in cast
g god wetter .
IH

15 A SPANISH ACCOUNT

Captain Luis de Cordoba was one of the very few Spaniards wrecked on the Irish coast who survived to return home. His narrative of the campaign from the Spanish point of view was given to his English interrogators.

The examinac[i]on of Don Lewes de Cordua in Andolozia

Don Lewse de Cordua in Andolozia: Capten of the Companie cast on shoare in S[i]r Morogh ne doe his Contry[1], saieth upon his examinac[i]on, that when the Spanishe fleete came before Plymouthe they were 140 Saile of all sorts whereof iiij[xx] and xvj were greate shippes for the fight, and the rest were patasses[2] and small vessells for carriage, At which place they mett w[ith] 70 of the Quenes shippes or there abouts. The Quenes shippes gatt into the winde of them[3] and shott at them, they kepeing on theire marche towards Callice, answeared the shott which continewed about ij or iij howres, In which skirmishe Don Pedro and his shipp were taken, being throwen behinde his companie, by reason of a shott that brake his maine maste[4]. The next day was calme & therefore nothing don betwene them, but a shipp of 700 tonne was burned by negligence among the Spaniards, but most of her men saved. The 3[rd] daie they skirmished 5 or 6 howres w[ith]out any shipp lost. The 4[th] day they fought 4 howres w[ith]out any shipp lost. The 5[th] day they came before Callis, and there anchored & cheyned them selves, at which tyme there came to succor of the Quenes shippes 25 more[5]: And in the night they perceaved 6 shippes falling upon them fired[6]: by reason whereof they were dryven to cutt theire Cables and sett saile: att which tyme a greate shipp was burned among them[7], and a Galleas cast awaie on the sands. After which thenglishe shippes entred into a sharpe fyght w[i]t[h] them wherein 2 of theire greatest Galleons were so beaten, that they were dryven to come a shore upon fflaunders, or those parts havinge disburdened theire men in theire other shippes.[8] That day if the fire had not broken them they had determined to have putt 7000 men on shoare att Callis to have gon to the prince of Parma to have knowen further his pleasure, for that they were from thence to be directed by him and had some Com[m]ission unto him not opened att all but lost in the shipp that was there burnt, but being p[re]vented by the saide fire they were broken, and so fought w[ith]all and followed 3 dayes after that out of sight of the Coast, and that the Quenes shippes left them, & retorned shoteing off a greate vollue of ordinaunce for ioye. After this the Duke of Medina assembled all his forc[e]s that were lefte, and founde that he had lost but six shippes of all sorts. And then gave order for them to retorne to Spaine: But about Norway the greate tempest tooke them, & beate those men nowe prisoners to this Coaste, of which Coast the Duke had before geven them greate charge to take heede.

He saieth that in the Armye were many yong Dukes, and noble men venturers, but he knoweth nott theire names. He saieth touching him selfe that his elder brother is a gent[leman] of 1000 duckets p[er] Ann[u]m, & that him selfe is not of any lyveliehood he was imployed by the kinge as a gent[leman] at 30 Crownes p[er] mensem in Cicilia.[9] and sent for from thence by the kinge to s[er]ve in this expedition wherein he had charge of 100 men in this shipp that is cast a waie being a flemishe hulk called the white ffaulkon in which were no more souldiors but this hundred.

State Papers Ireland, 1588, SP 63/137 No.I,iii, f. 5

1 Sir Murrough ne Doe (ne d-tuadh), chief of the O'Flahertys of Galway.
2 Pataches, similar to the English pinnace.
3 i.e. gained the weather gage.
4 The *Nuestra Senora del Rosario,* flagship of Pedro de Valdes, lost her foremast as a result of a collision.
5 Seymour's squadron from the Downs.
6 Actually eight fireships.
7 In fact no ship was burned.
8 Most of the men of these two ships were still aboard when they grounded, and were subsequently massacred by the Dutch.
9 Sicily; he was a company commander in the Sicilian *tercio* or regiment.

The examinaton of Don Lewes de Cordua
in Andolozia.

Don Lewse de Cordua in Andolozia: Capten of the Companie that on shoare
in Emonyth nere to his Contry, saith, vpon his examinaton, that when
the Spanishe fleete came before Plymonthe they were 140. Saile of
all sorte, whereof iiij. and xx. were greate shippes for the fight, and
the rest were patasses and smale vessells for carriage, At which
place they mett w 70. of the Quenes shippes or there abonte. The
Quenes shippes gatt into the winde of them and shott at them, they
kepeing on theire marche towarde Callice, answeared the shott which
contineued about ij. or iij howres, In which skirmishe Don Pedro
and his shipp were taken, being throwen behind his companie, by
reason of a shott that brake his maine maste. The next day
was calme & therefore nothing don betwene them, but a shipp of
700. tonne was burned by negligence among the Spaniardes, but
most of her men saved. The 3 daie they skirmished. 5. or 6.
howres w out any shipp lost. The 4. day they fought 4. howres
w out any shipp lost. The 5. day they came before Callice, and
there anchored & reposed them selves, at which tyme there came
to succor of the Quenes shippes. 25. more: And in the night they
perceaved. 6. shippes falling vpon them fired: by reason whereof
they were dryven to cutt theire cables and sett saile: at which
tyme a greate shipp was burned among them, and a Galleass cast
awaie on the sande. After which, thenglishe shippes entred into
a scharpe fight w them wherein 2. of theire greatest Galleons
were so beaten, that they were dryven to come a shoare vpon
fflannders, or those parte having disburdened theire men in
theire other shippes. That day if the fire had not broken them
they had determined to have gonne 7000. men on shoare att Callice
to have gon to the prince of Parma to have knowen further
his pleasure, for that they were from thence to be directed by him
and had some comission vnto him not opened att all but lost in
the shipp that was there burnt, but being prevented by the saide fire
they were broken, and so fought w all and followed. 3. dayes after
that out of sight of the coast, and that the Quenes shippes left
them, returned shoting of a greate volue of ordinaunce for ioye.
After this the Duke of Medina: assembled all his forte that were
lefte, and founde that he had lost but sixe shippes of all sorte.
And then gave order for them to returne to Spaine: But about
Norway the greate tempest tooke them, & beate those men nowe
prisoners to this coast, of which coast the Duke had before

(marginal notes:)
140. saile
a forbonyd / y Galyas / 2. Galleasse
vnt 6.

yeven them greate charge to take heede.

He saith that in the Armye were many yong Dukes and
noble men venturers, but he knoweth not theire names.

He saith touching him selfe that his elder brother is a gent.
of 1000 Dukets of Rennt. & that him selfe is not of any Lyvelich od
he was imployed by the Kinge as a gent. at 30 Crownes of
messes in Cicilia. and sent for from thence by the Kinge to
serve in this Expedition wherein he hath charge of 100 men in
this Shipp that is cast a waie being a Flemish hulk called
the Whit ffalcon in which were no more souldiors but
this hundred.

a flemish
whyt falco

The Copie of Sr Ry: Binghm
his lre to the Lord Deputie.

1588.

68

This translation of Medina Sidonia's sailing instructions for the Armada's return to Spain was probably obtained from a prisoner interrogated in Ireland.

Dyrection geven by the Duke of Medyna for the Course w[hi]c[h] the Spaynishe Navy should hould on their retorne to Spayne.

The Course that shalbe held in the retorne of this Army[1] into Spayne:

The Course that is first to be held, is to the north north-east untill you be found under 61 degrees & a halph[2]: And then to take great hede least you fall upon the Iland of Ireland for feare of the harme that may happen unto you upon that Coast: Then p[ar]ting from those Ilands and doubling the cape in 61 degrees & a halph you shall comme west Southwest untill you be found under 58 degrees And from thence to the South west to the height of 53 degrees & then to the South southwest making to the Cape finest[err]e & so to procure yo[u]r entraunce into the Groyne or to fferroll or to any other port of [the] Cost of Gallisia.

State Papers Ireland, 1588, Sp 63/137 No.I,ii, f. 4
1   The literal translation of Armada.
2   Degrees of north latitude.

The course that shalbe held in the returne
of this Army into Spayne

The course that is first to be held, is to the north northe
east untill yo be found under. 61. degrees & a halfe: And
then to take great hede least yo fall upon the Iland of
Irelande for feare of the harme that may happen unto yo
upon that coast: Then plying from those Ilands and
doubling the ryse in. 61. degrees & a halfe yo shall runne
most Southwest untill yo be found under. 58. degrees
And from thence to the Southwest to the height of
53. degrees & then to the South southwest making
to the Cape finester & so to governe yo entering into
the Groyne or to Ferroll or to any other part of
coast of Gallisia.

17 SHIPWRECK IN IRELAND

Alonso de Leiva was one of the most distinguished senior officers of the Armada, and a favourite of King Philip's. James Machary was lucky to be left behind when he sailed from Killybegs: the Gerona was wrecked on the coast of Ulster with the loss of de Leiva and almost all on board.

The examinac[i]on of James Machary of the Crosse w[i]t[h]in the Countie of Typperary, taken before the right honorable the Lo[rd] deputie[1] the 29 day of December 1588.

He saieth he was imprest at Lysbon in Spaine, and put into a fflemyshe hulcke called St.Ann of the burden of 400 and better in which were 300 souldiors, and 150 mariners, and the rest of the loading being victualls. After the fight in the narrowe Seas she fell upon the Coast of Ireland in a haven called Erris St.Donnell[2]. where at theire cominge in they found a greate shipp called the Rat[3] of 1000 tonn, or rather a good deale more, in which was Don Alonso de Leva: and an Erle called Counte De Paris:[4] and a brother of the same Erle, also a gent[leman] named Don Thomaso de gran Bello[5]: a man much favored w[i]t[h] the K[ing] of greate revennewe, and a naturall Spa[niard] borne, w[i]th dyvers good Captens and other gallant gent[leman]. there was in this shipp of all sorts above 700.

After she perished, Don Alonso and all his companie were receaved into the hulcke of St.Ann w[i]t[h] all the goods they had in the shipp of any valewe, as plate, apparell, monie, iewells, weapons, armor &c leaving behind them victuall, Ordinaunce, and much other stuffe which the hulcke was not hable to carie away: which don they sett the shipp on fire, and made saile for Spaine, in which course by a contrarie wynde they were dryven back upon mc Swine ny does[6] Cuntrie to a place called Longherris[7], where falling to Ankor, there fell a greate storme which brake in sonder all theire Cables, and strooke them upon grounde, whereby Don Alonso and all his companie were enforced to goe on shoare taking all theire goods, and armor w[i]th them, and there by the shipp side incamped them selves for the space of 8 or 9 daies.

Don Alonso before he came to Lande was hurte in the legge by the Capstele[8] of the shipp in such sorte as he was nether hable to goe nor ride, nether duering the 9 daies of his incampinge, nor upon his remove, but was carried from that place, to the place[9] wherein the Gallias (named Gerona lay) betwene 4 men, being 19 myles distaunce, where likewise he and all his companie incamped 12 or 14 daies in which tyme the Gallias was finished, and made readie for the sea as well as she could be: He being advertised certenly from tyme to tyme that the Lo[rd] deputie was preparing him selfe to come against them, put him self aboorde her, having for his pilott 3 Irishe men and a Scott. There was in the Gallias of her owne souldiors (besids 300 slaves) 5 or 600 men.

He saieth that Don Alonso, for his stature was tawle and slender, of a whitly complexion, of a flaxen and smothe heare, of behaviour mylde and temperate, of speeche good and deliberate, greatly reverencid not only of his owne men, but generally of all the whole companie. And thus being all shipped in the saide Gallias he saieth they departed for Scotland, but what became of them this examin[an]t cannot saie.

State Papers Ireland, SP 63/139 No.25,i, f. 83
1 Sir William Fitzwilliams, Lord Deputy of Ireland and head of the English government in that country.
2 Blacksod Bay, on the coast of Erris.
3 *La Rata Coronada*.
4 The Count of Paredes.
5 Don Tomaso de Granvelle.
6 McSweeney ne Doe, (na d-Tuath), an underchief of the Earl of Tirconnel.
7 Loughros More Bay, Donegal.
8 Capstan.
9 Killybegs, Donegal.

The examinaton of James Machary of the Crosse
win the Countie of Typperary, taken before the
right honorable the Lo: Deputie the 29 day of
December 1588

He saieth he was imprest at Lysbon in Spaine, and put into a
Flemmyshe hulke called the St Ann of the burden of 400 and better
in which were 300 souldiers, and 150 marinors, and the rest of the
loadinge beinge virtualls. After the fight in the narrowe seas
she fell vpon the Coast of Ireland in a haven called Erris St Donnell
where at theire comeing in they found a greate shipp called the east
of 1000 tonn, or rather a good deale more, in which was Don Alonso
de Leua: and an Erle called Counte De Paris: and a brother of the
same Erle: also a gent named Don Thomaso de gran Bello: a man
much favored of the k: of greate revennewe; and a naturall Spa-
borne, wth dyvers good Captens and other gallant gent: There
was in this shipp of all sorts above 700.

After she perished, Don Alonso: and all his companie were receaved
into the hulke of St Ann wth all the goods they had in the shipp of
any valewe, as plate, apparell, monie, iewells, weapons, armor of:
leavinge behinde them virtuall, Ordinaunce, and much other stuffe
which the hulke was not hable to carrie away: which, Don then
sett the shipp on fire, and made saile for Spaine, in which
course by a contrarie wynde they were dryven back vpon the
coast in Iock Countrie to a place called Lonyhewis, where falling
to Anker, there fell a greate storme which brake in sonder all theire
Cables, and strooke them vpon grownde, whereby Don Alonso: and
all his companie were enforced to goe on shoare taking all theire
goods, and armor wth them, and there by the shipp side inramped
them selves for the space of 8 or 9 daies.

Don Alonso: before he came to Lande was hurte in the legge by the
Capesten of the shipp in such sorte as he was nether hable to goe
nor ride, nether dureing the 9 daies of his inrampinge, nor vpon his
remove, but was carried from that place to the place wherein the
Gallias named Gerona lay) betwene 4 men, beinge 19 myles distance,
where likewise he and all his companie inramped 12 or 14 daies in
which tyme the Galliaz was finished, and made readie for the
sea as well as she could be: He being advertised certenly from tyme
to tyme that the Lo: Deputie was preparing him selfe to come against
them, put him selfe aboorde her, havinge for his pilott 3 Irishe men
and a Scott. There was in the Galliaz of her owne souldiors
besides 300 slaves) 5 or 600 men.

He saieth that Don Alonso, for his stature was tawle and slender, of a
whitly complexion, of a flaxen and smothe heare, of behavior mylde
and temperate, of speeche good and deliberate, greatly reverenced
not only of his owne men, but generally of all the whole companie.
And thus being all shipped in the same Galliaz he saieth they
departed for Scotland, but what became of them this examin cannot
saie.

INDEX

Printed in the United Kingdom for Her Majesty's Stationery Office
Dd 238643 4/88 C40 3933/1 12521